This book is dedicated to my beloved mother ♡

Olga Goloveshkina

Chinchillum
botanicum

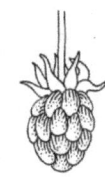

COLORING BOOK

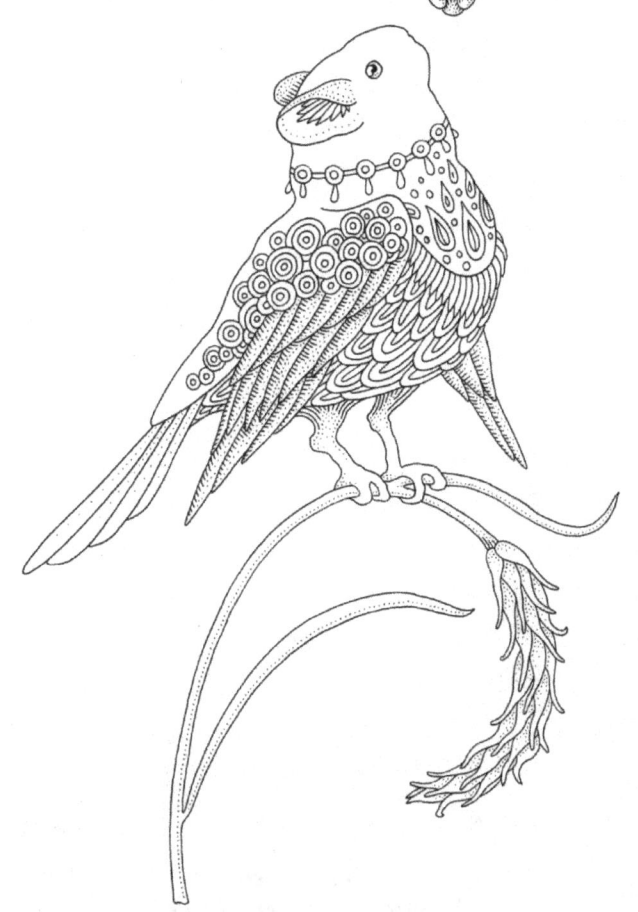

ISBN:172341350X
ISBN-13:9781723413506

This book belongs to

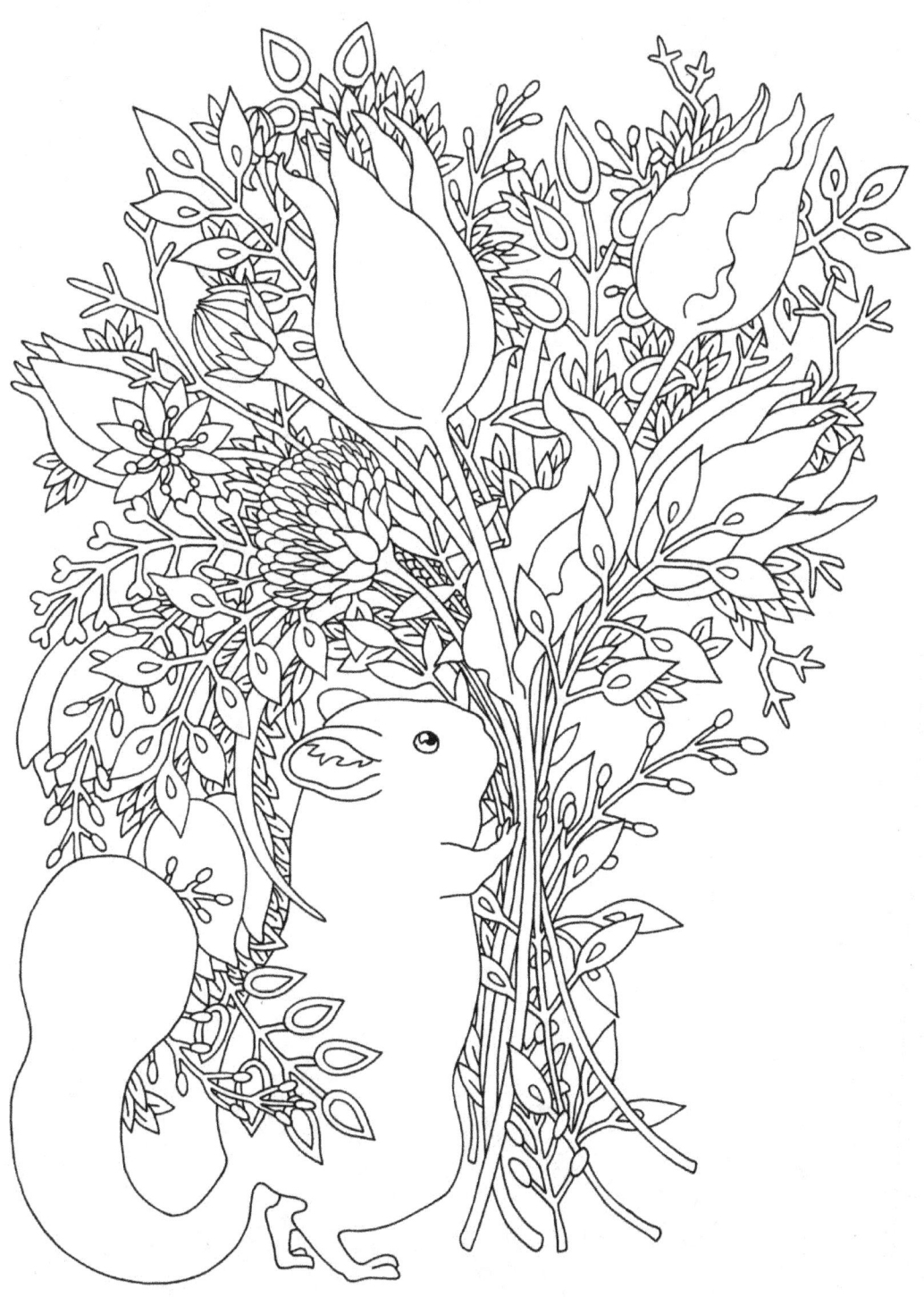

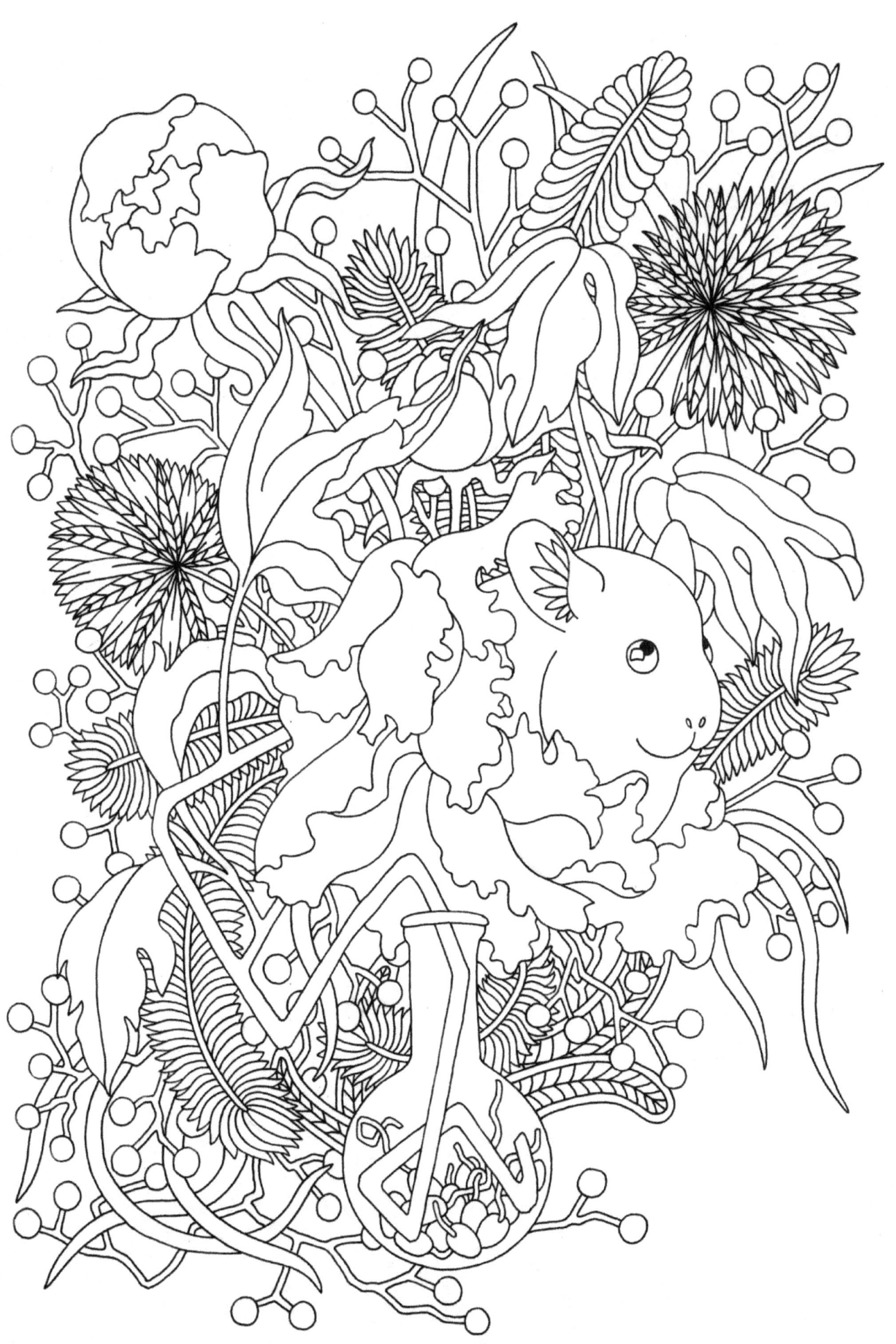

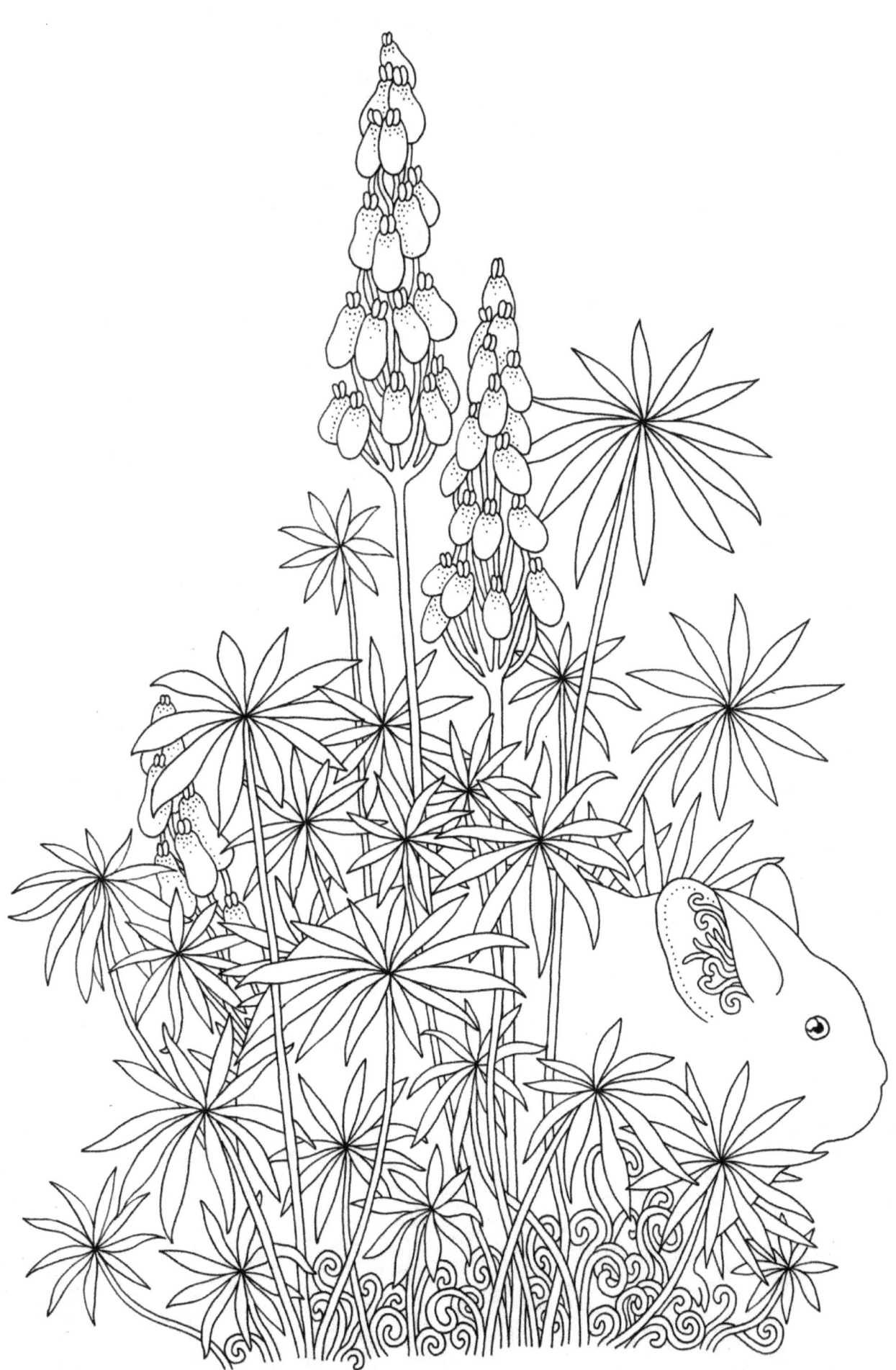

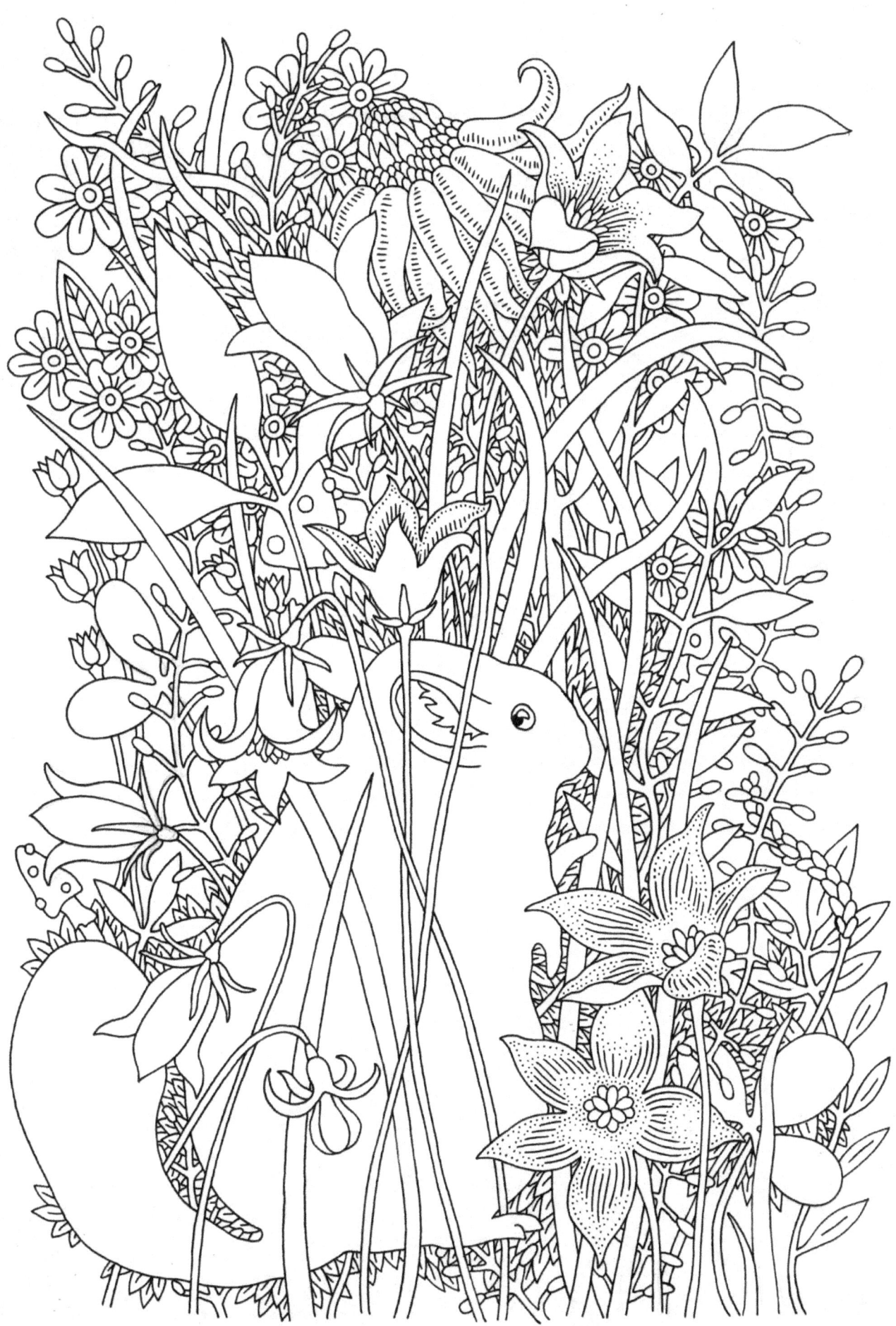

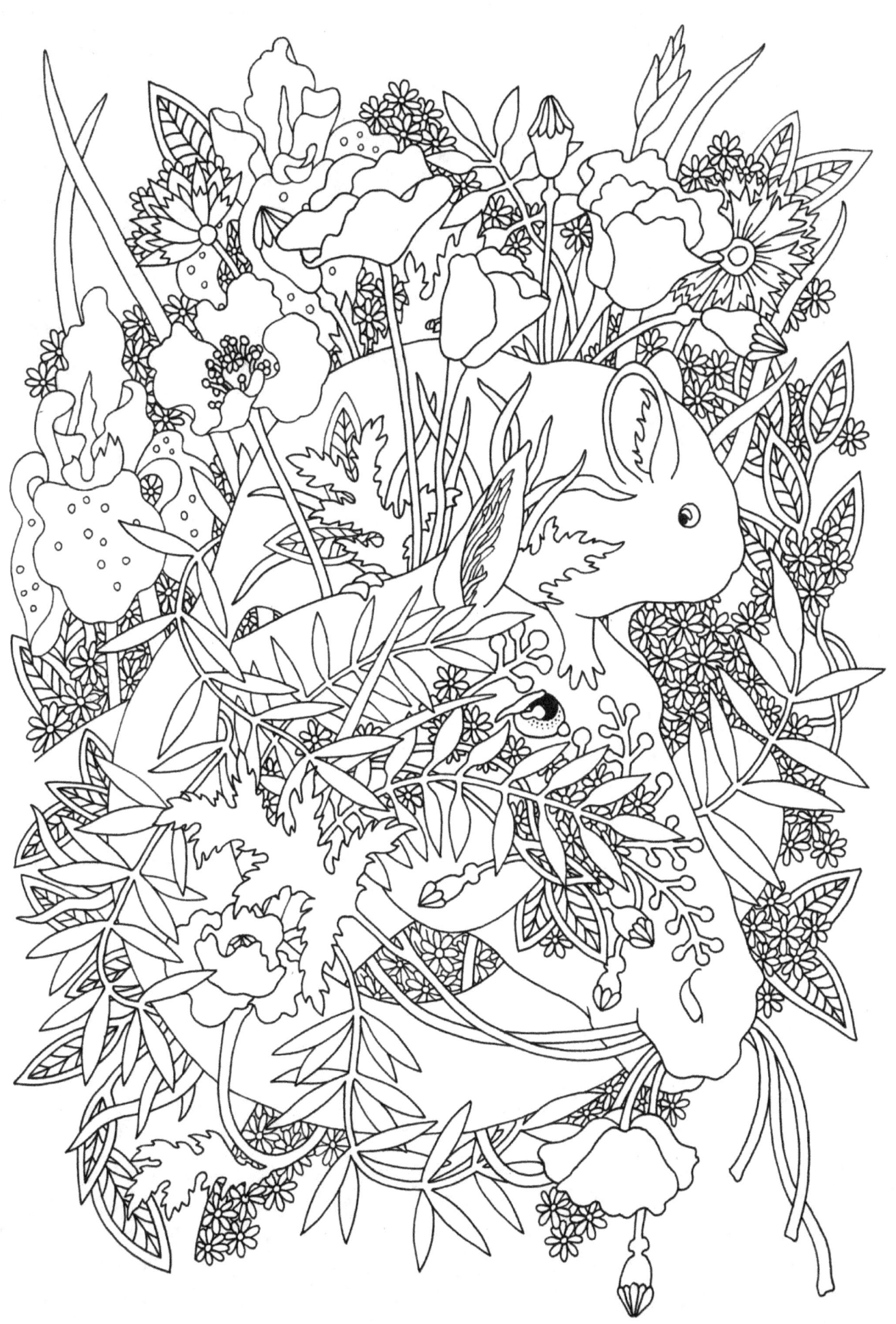

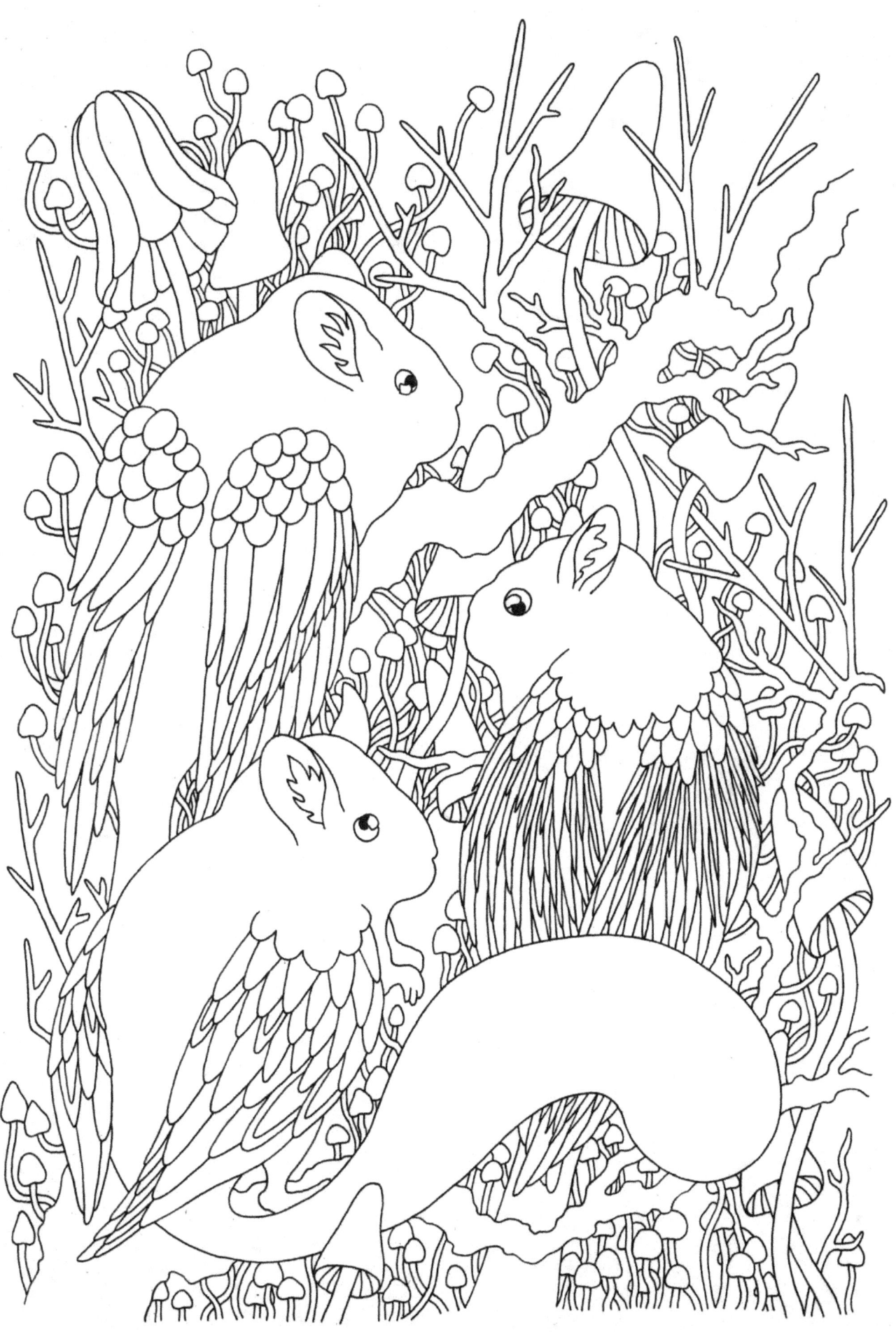

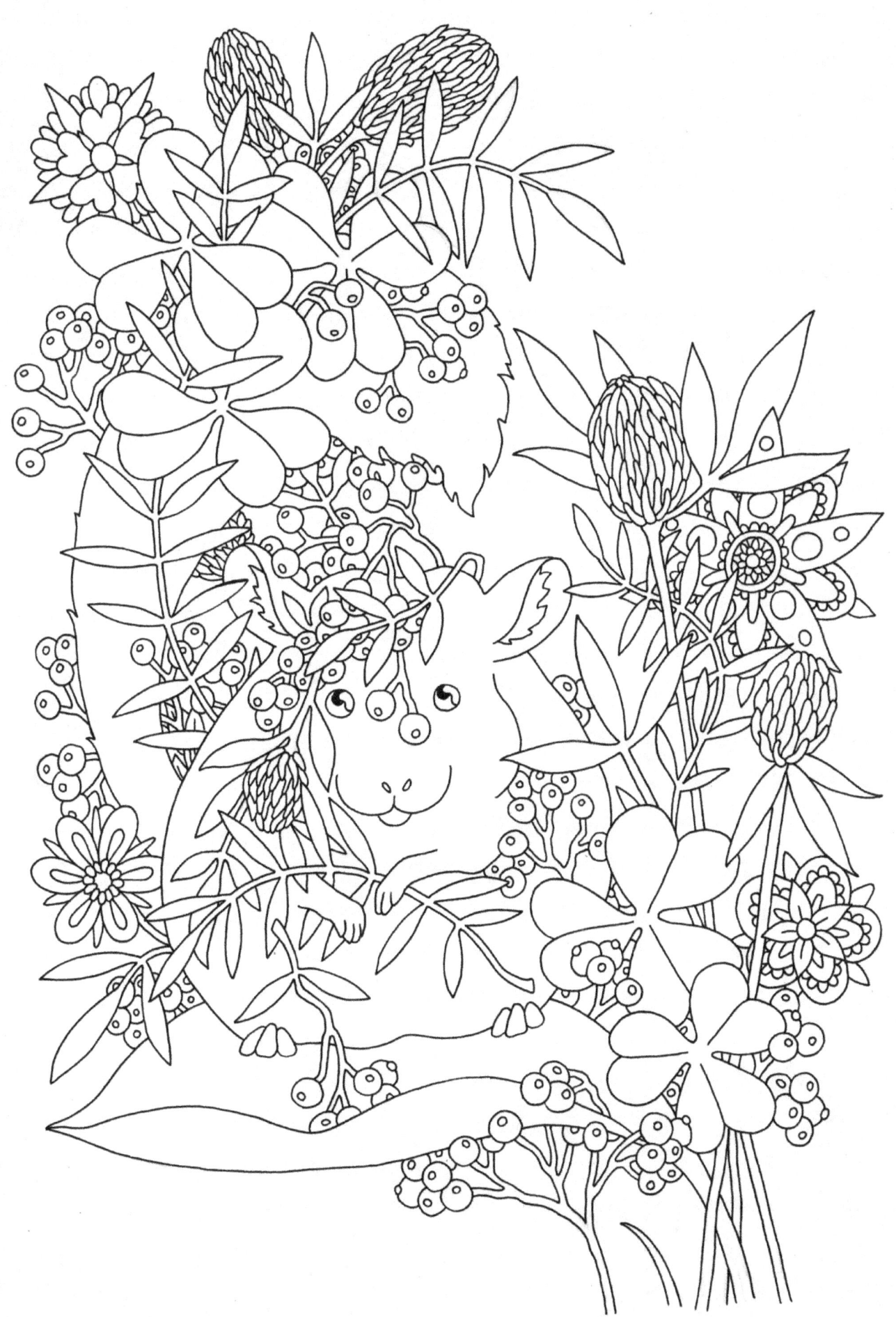

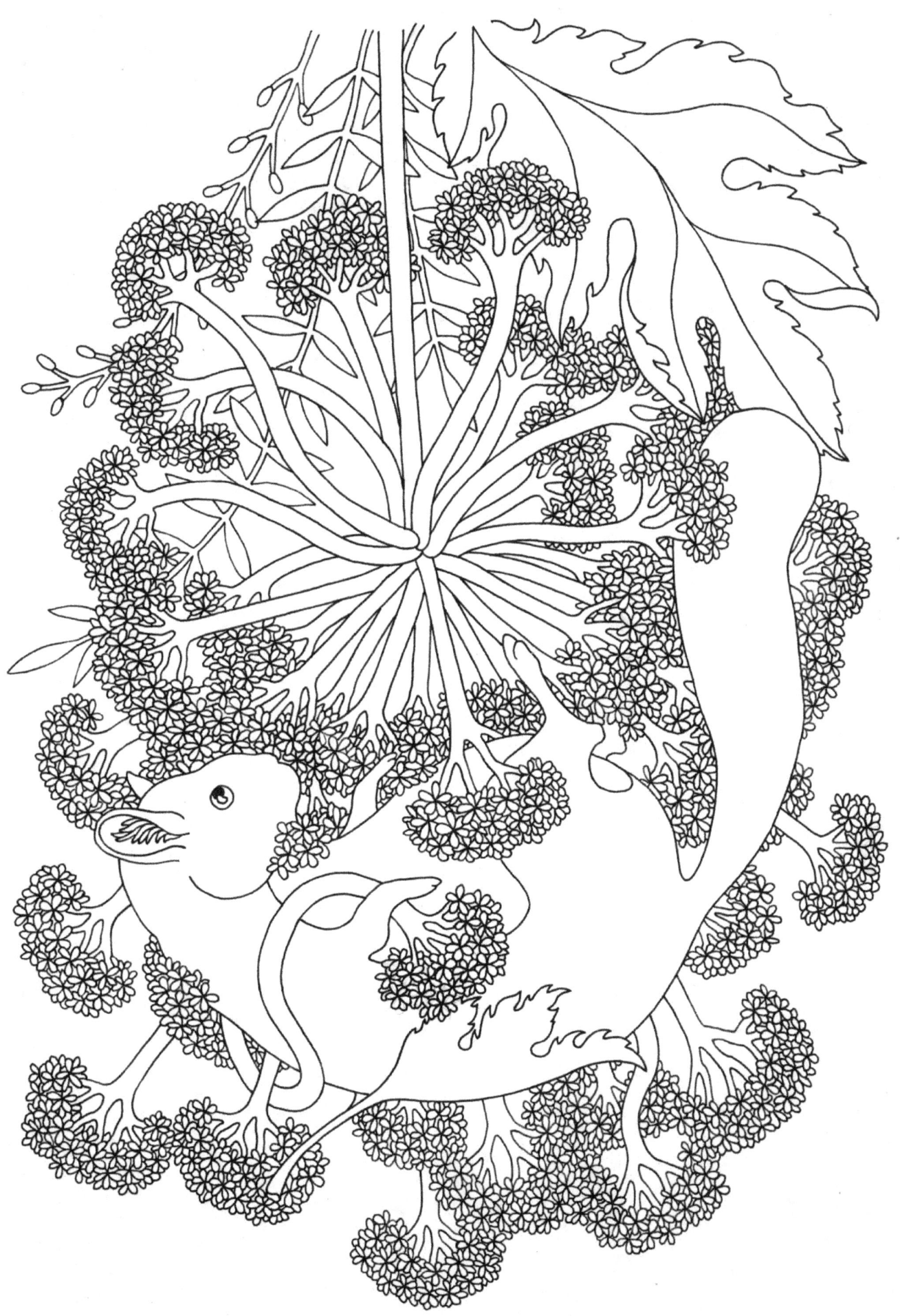

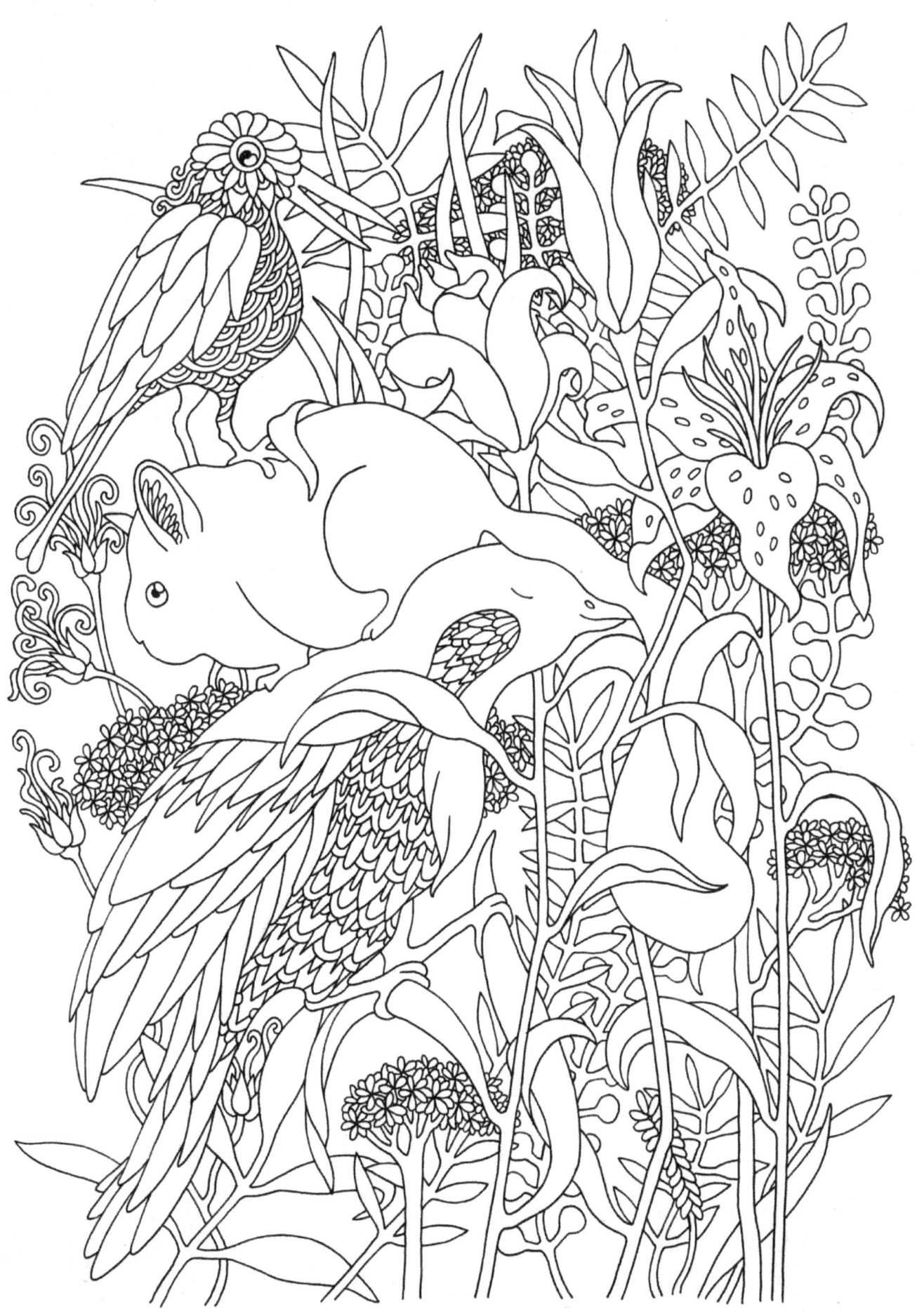

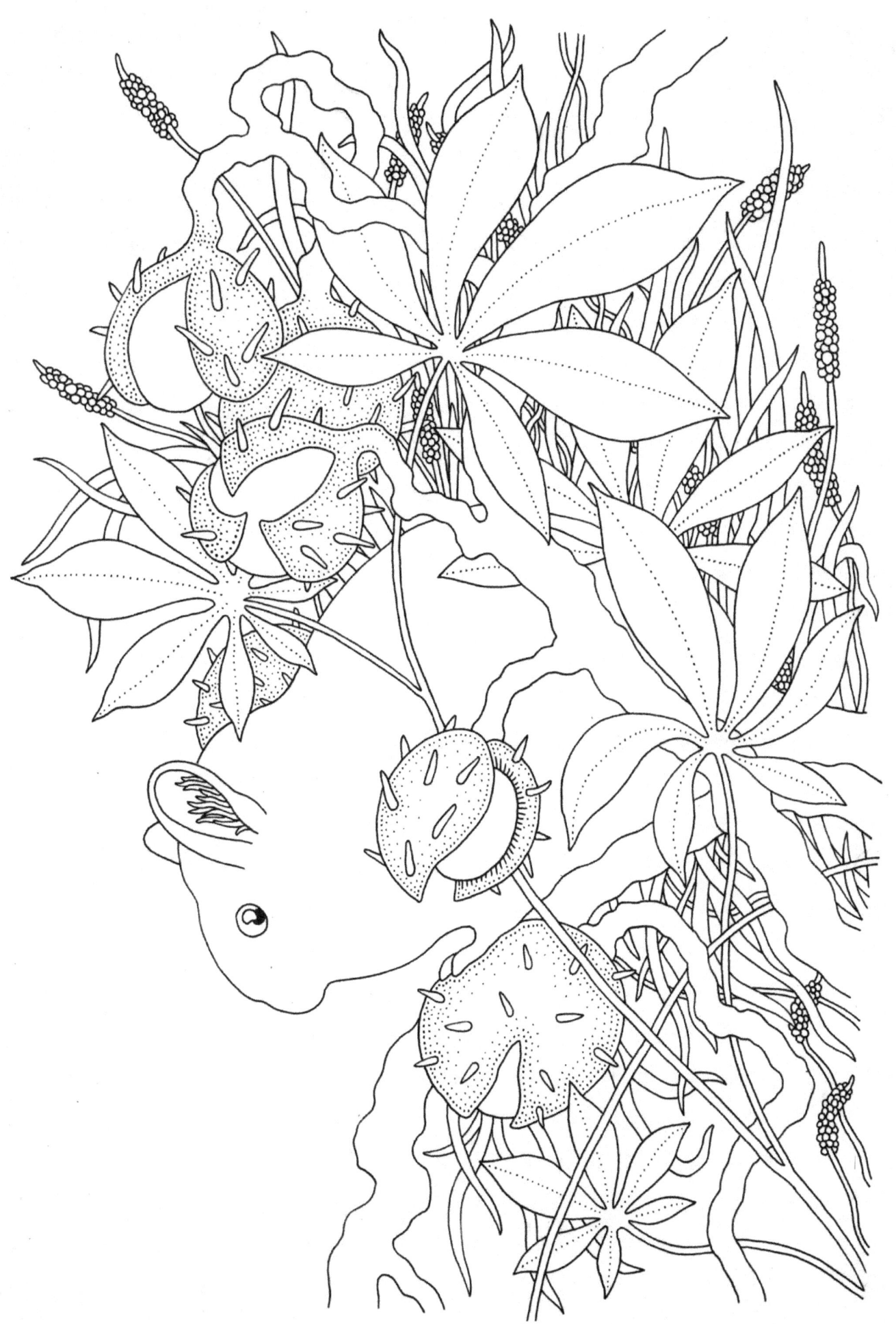

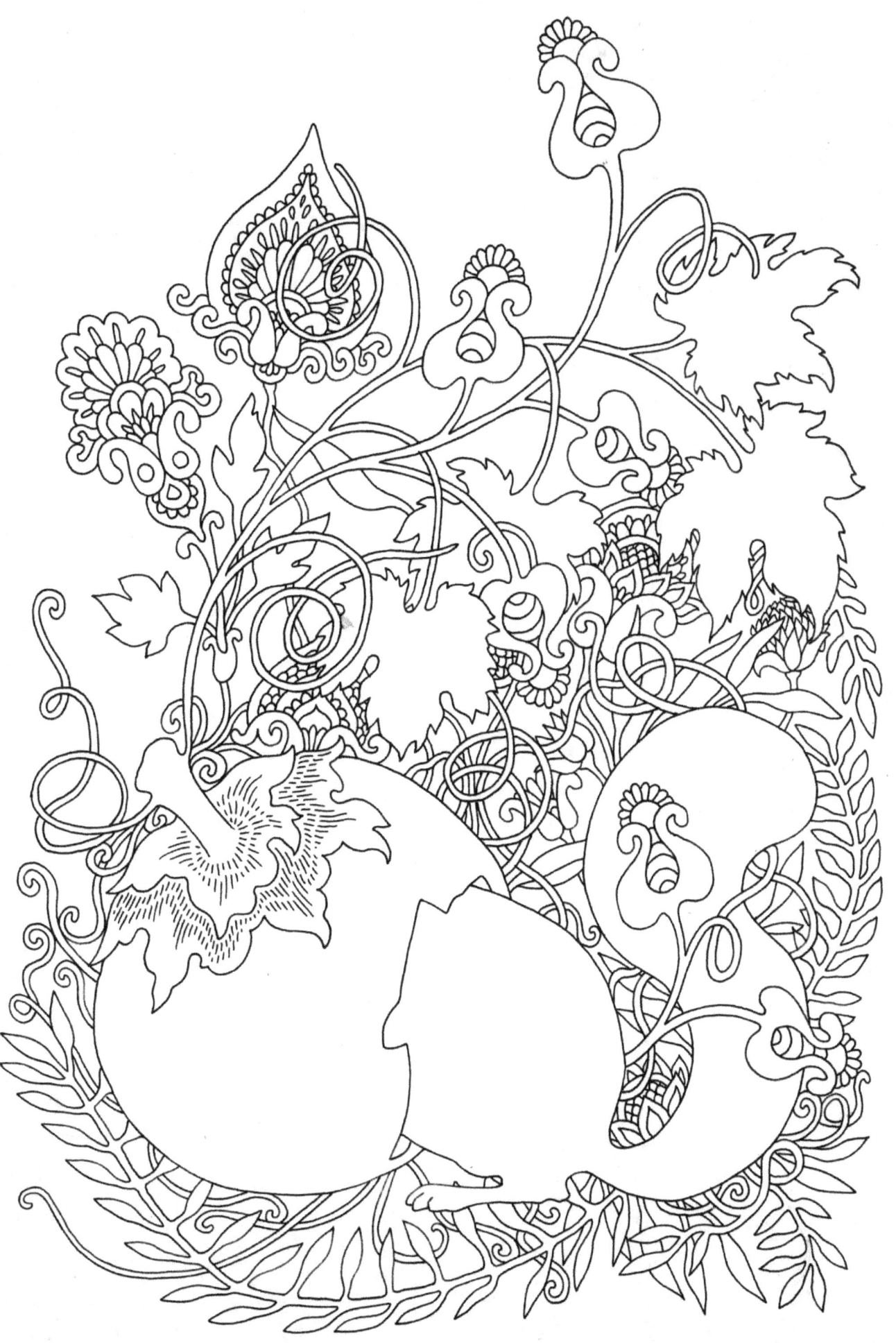

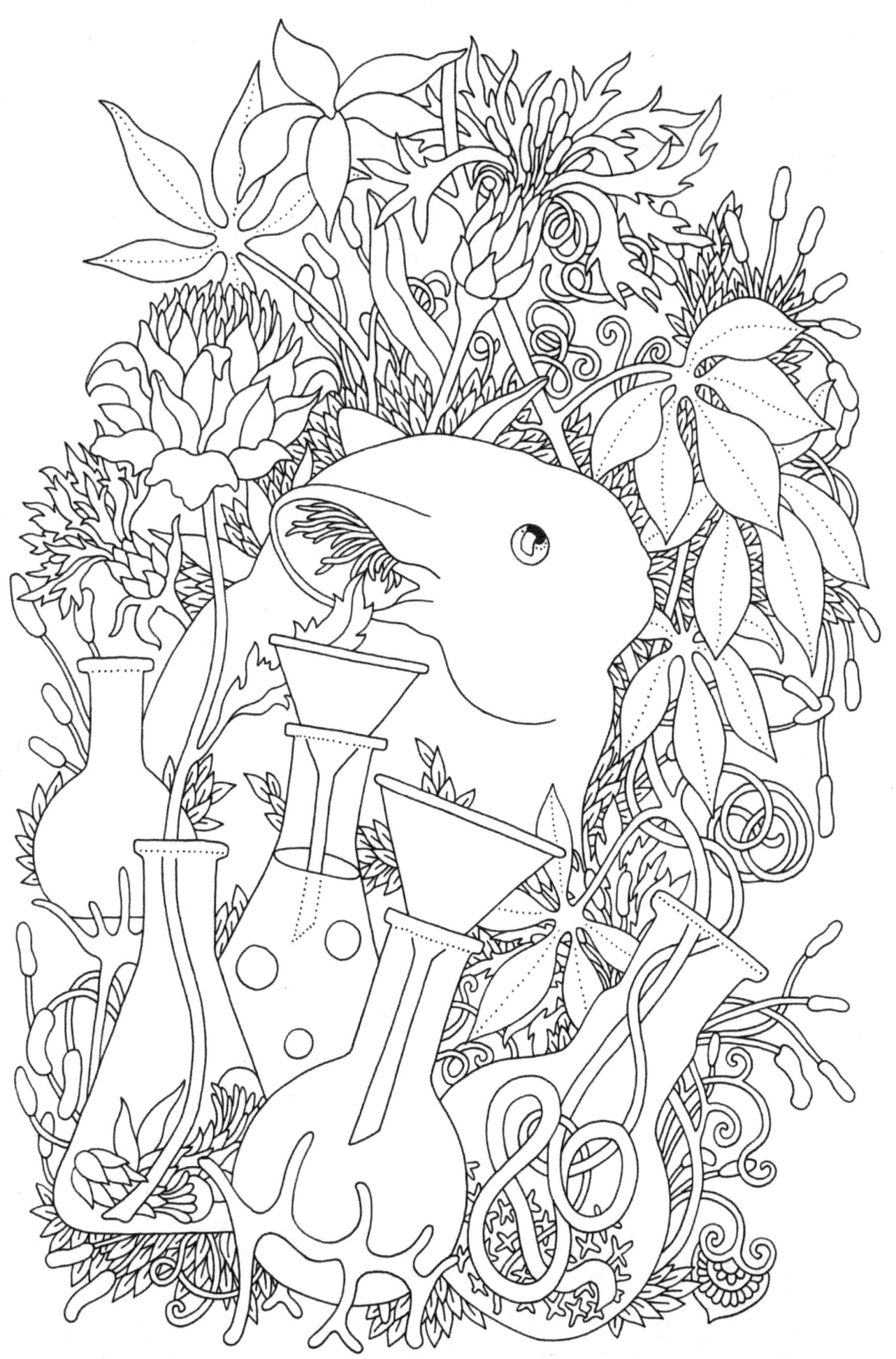

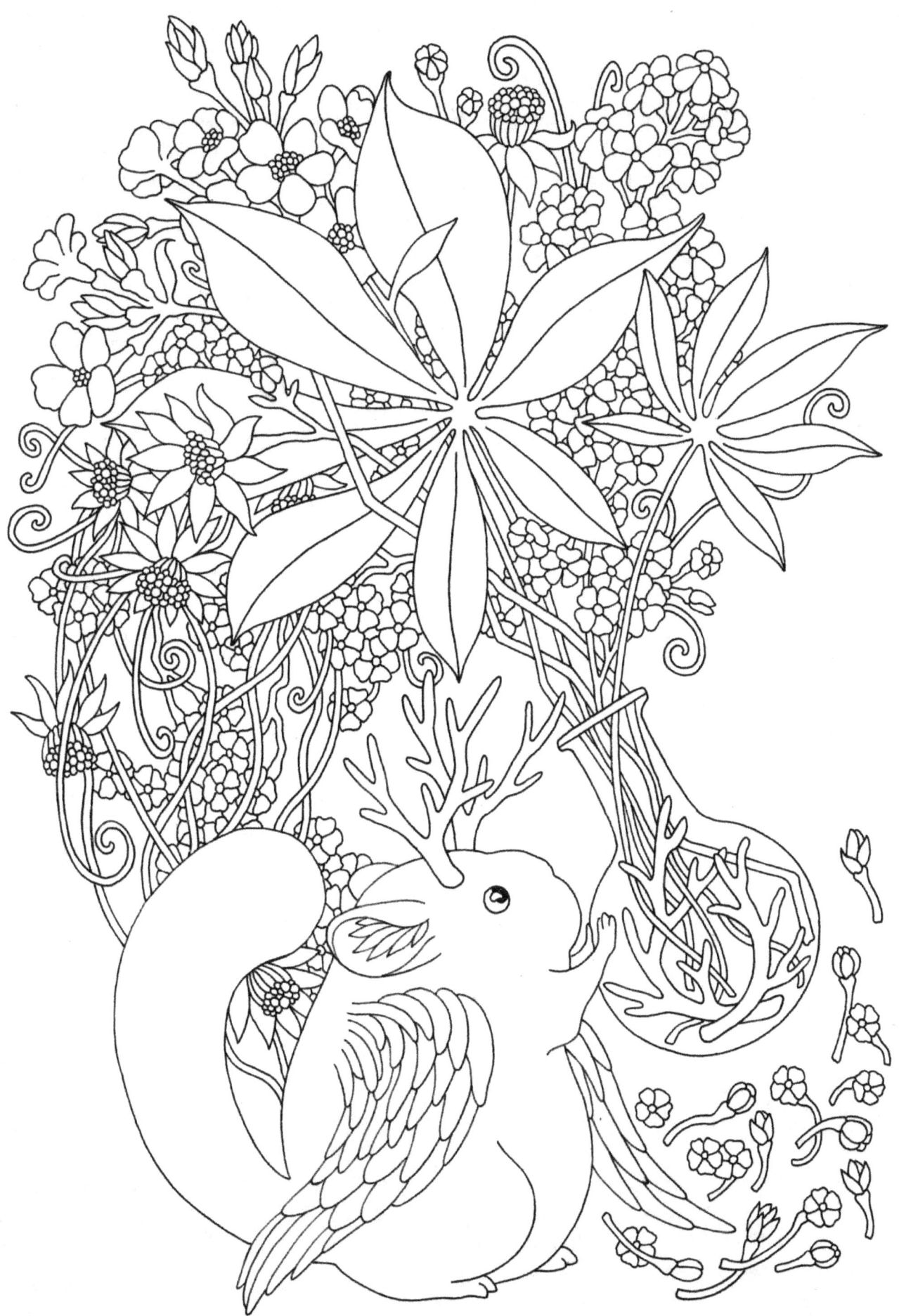

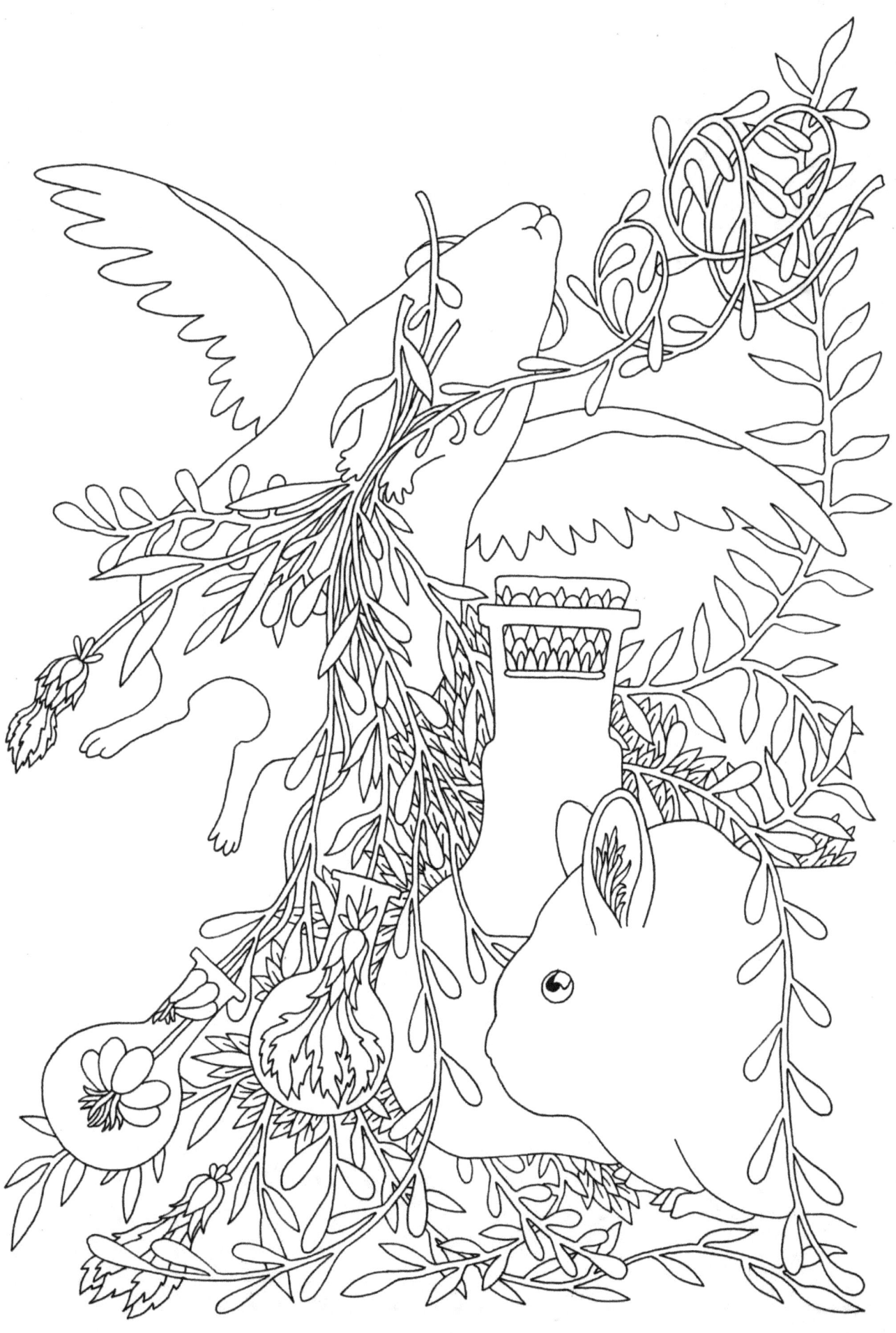

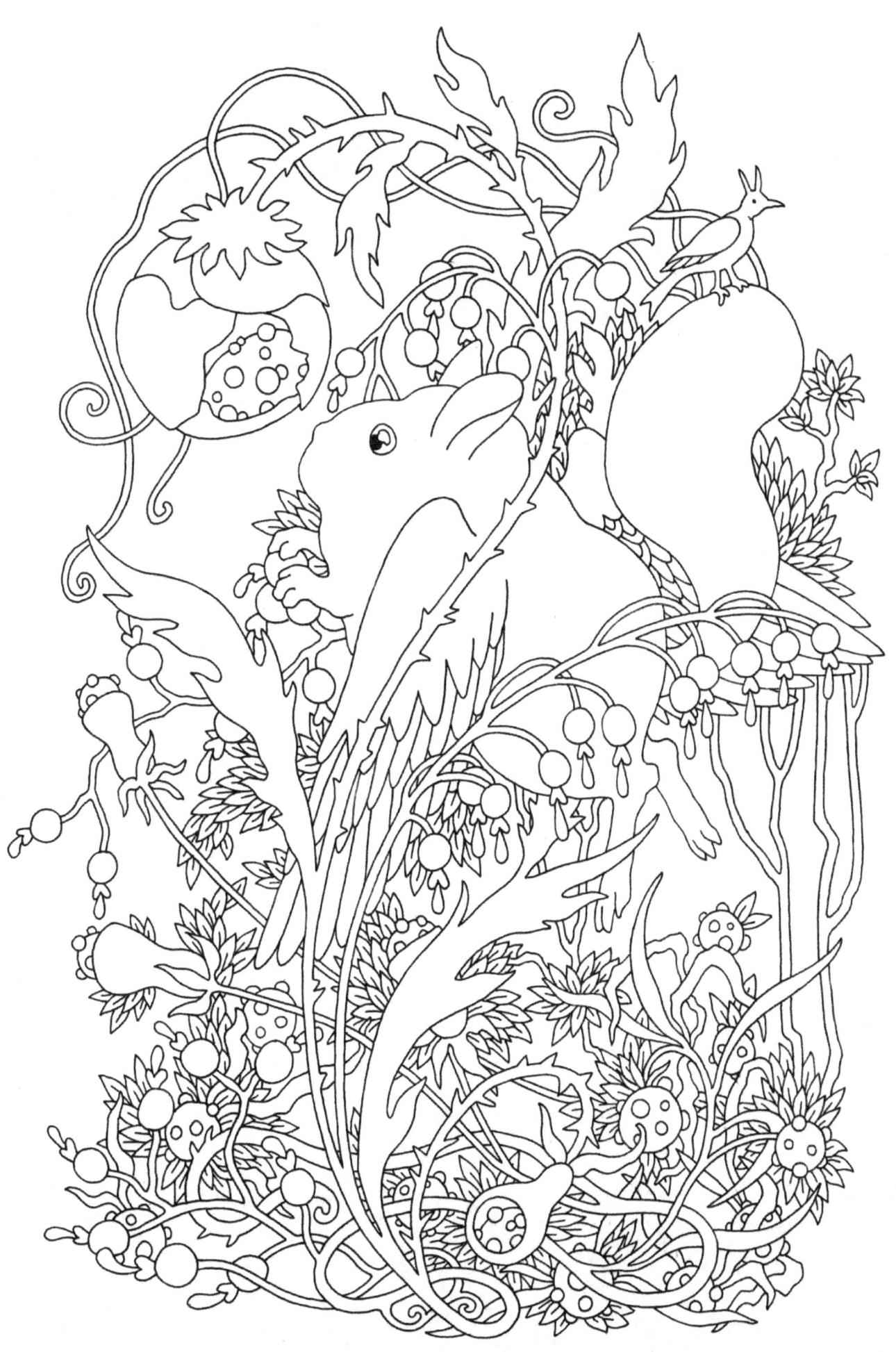

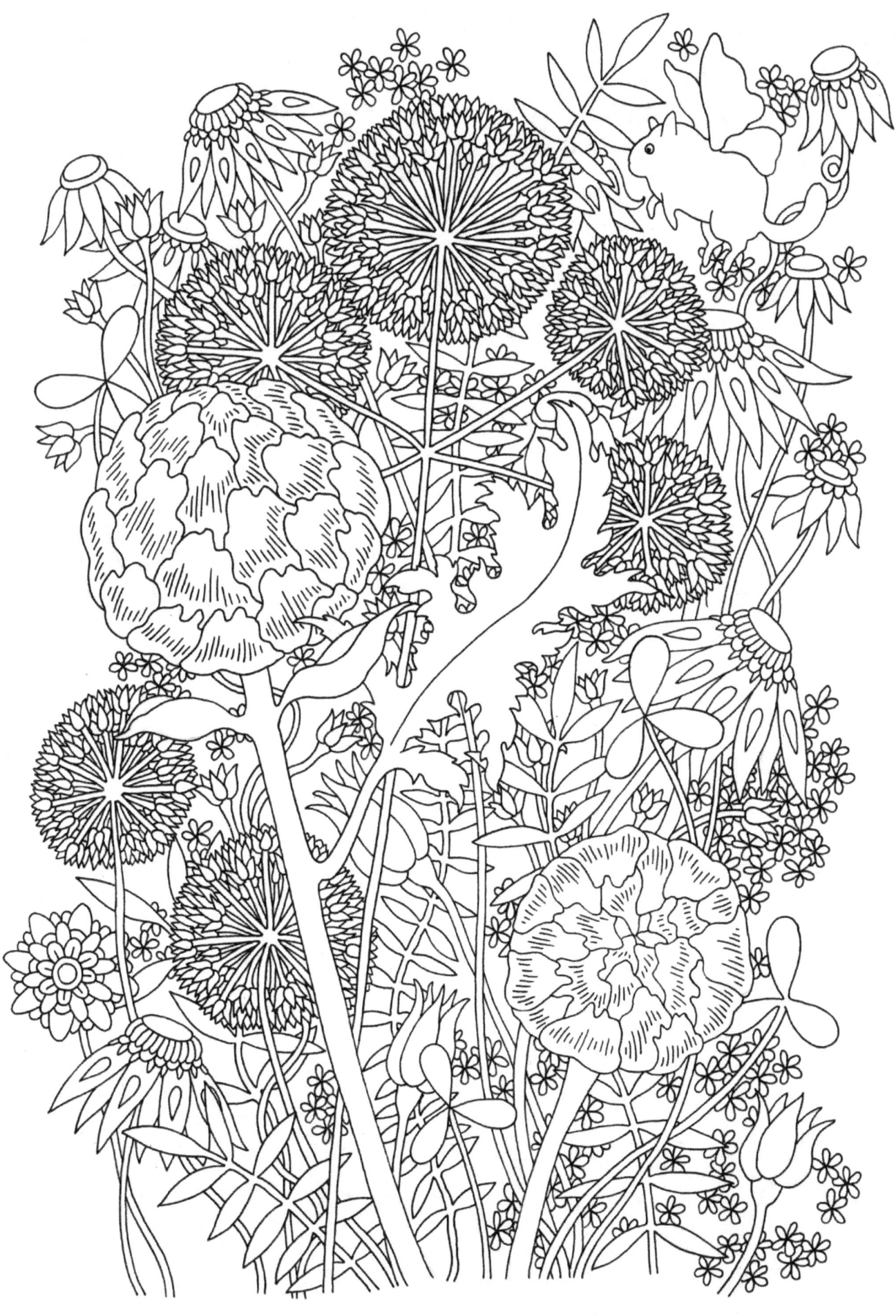

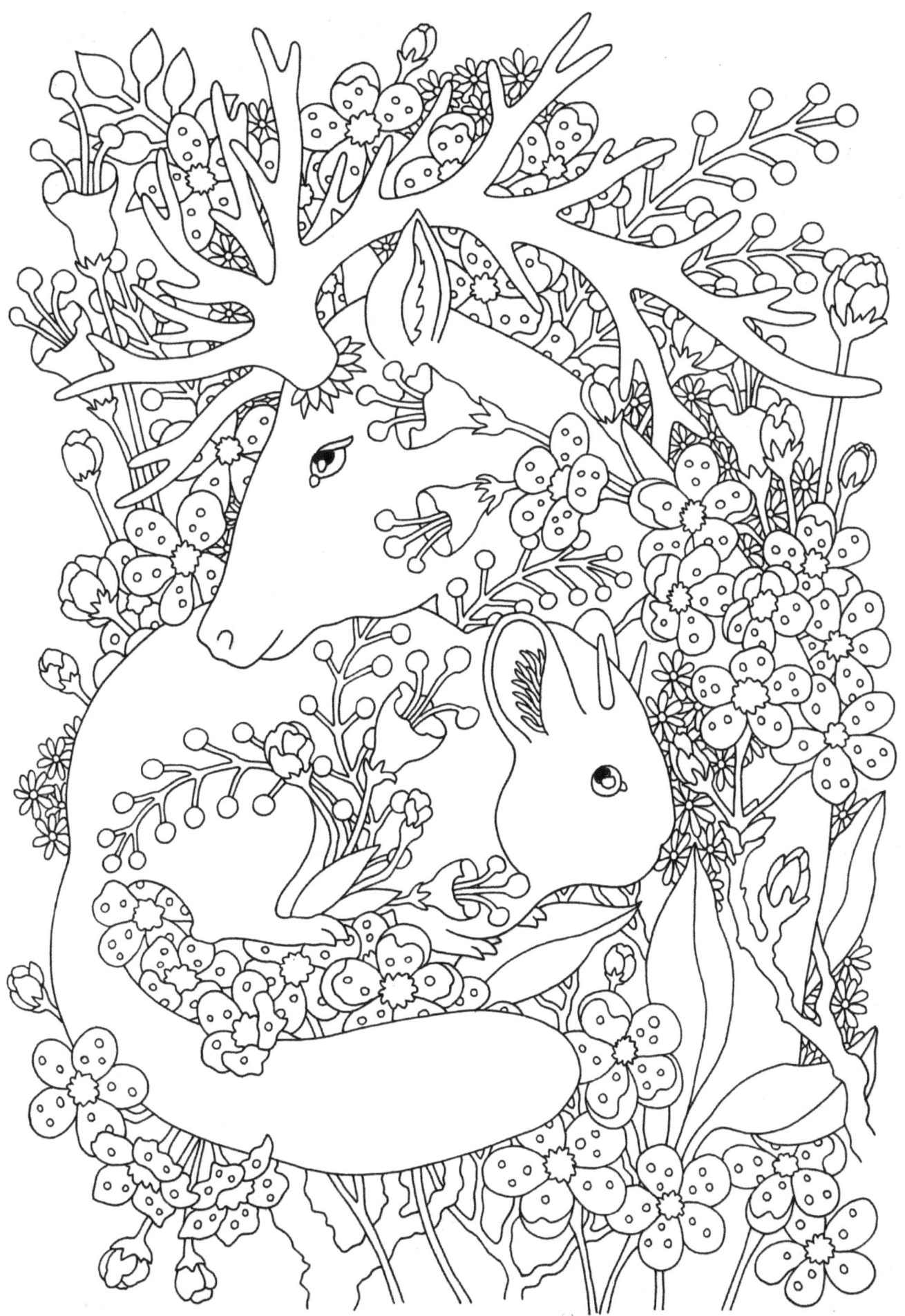

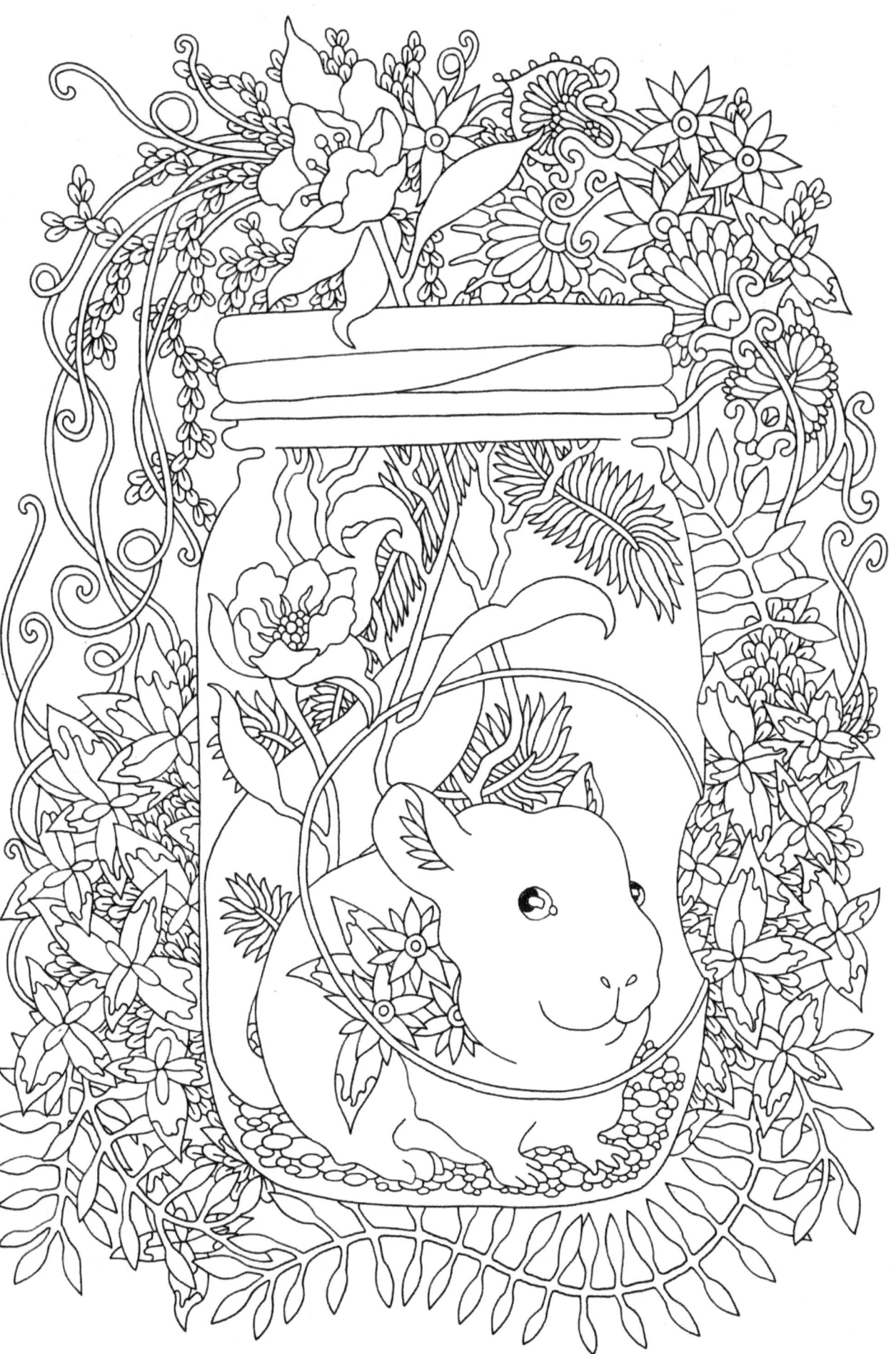

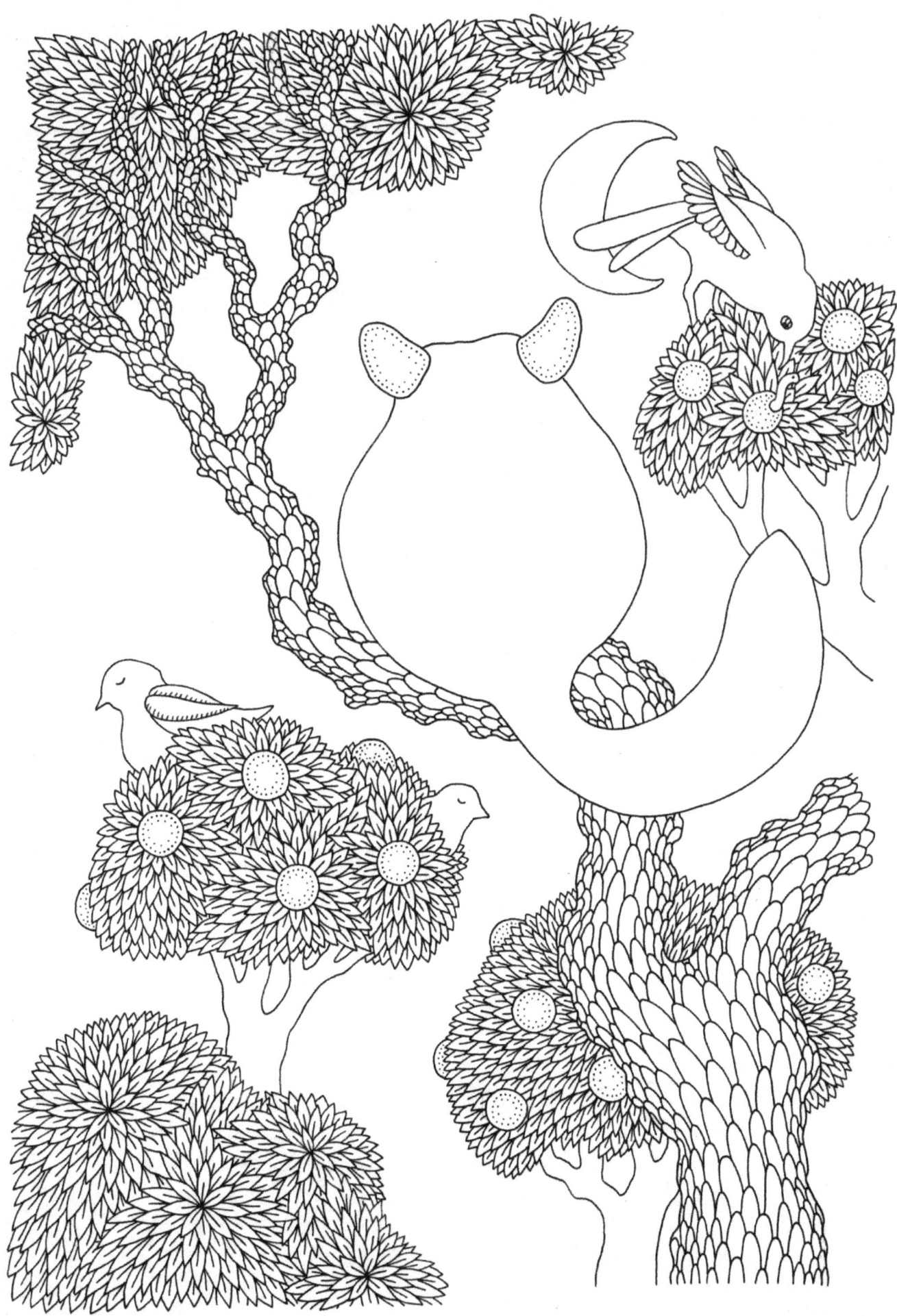

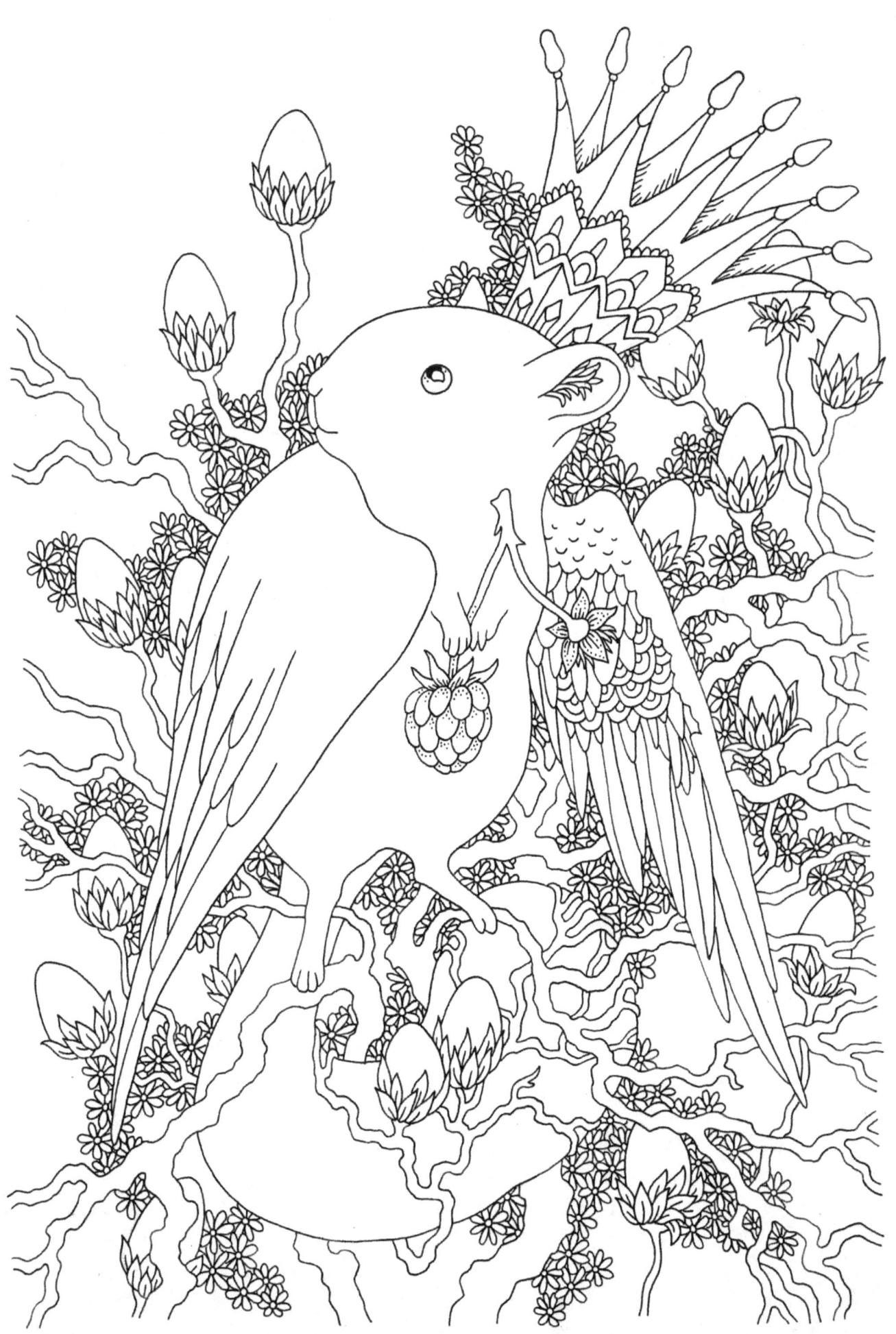

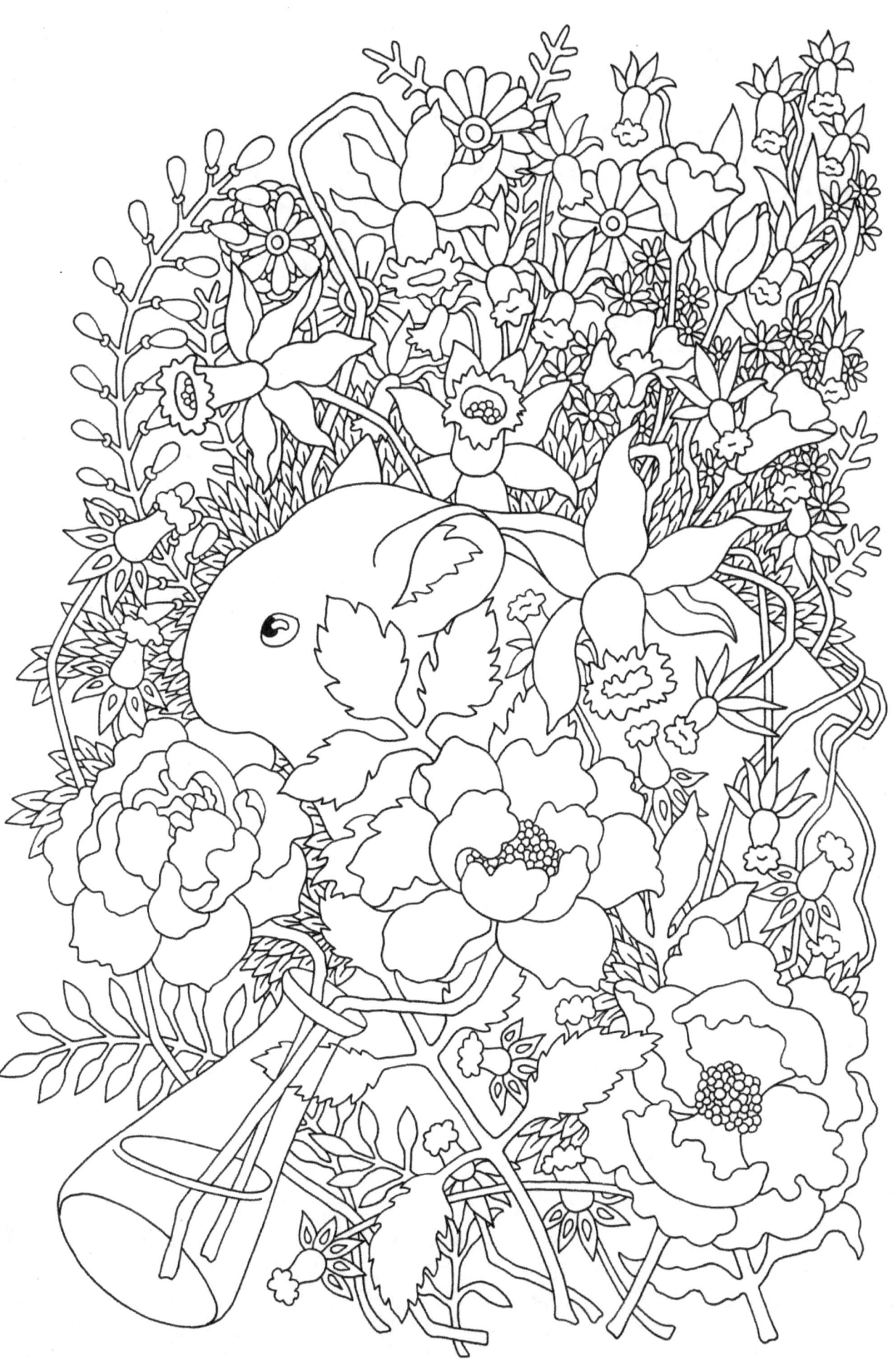

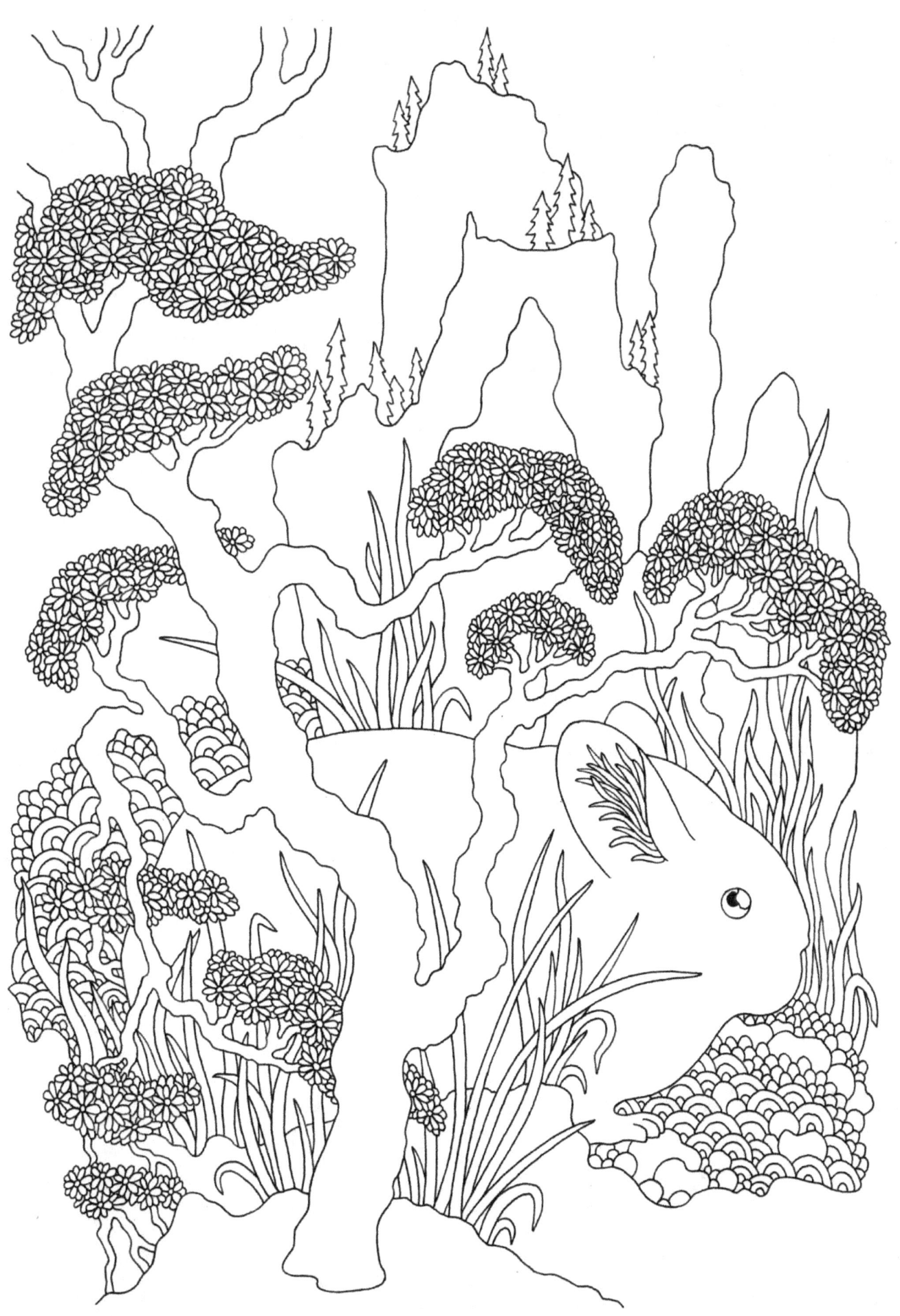

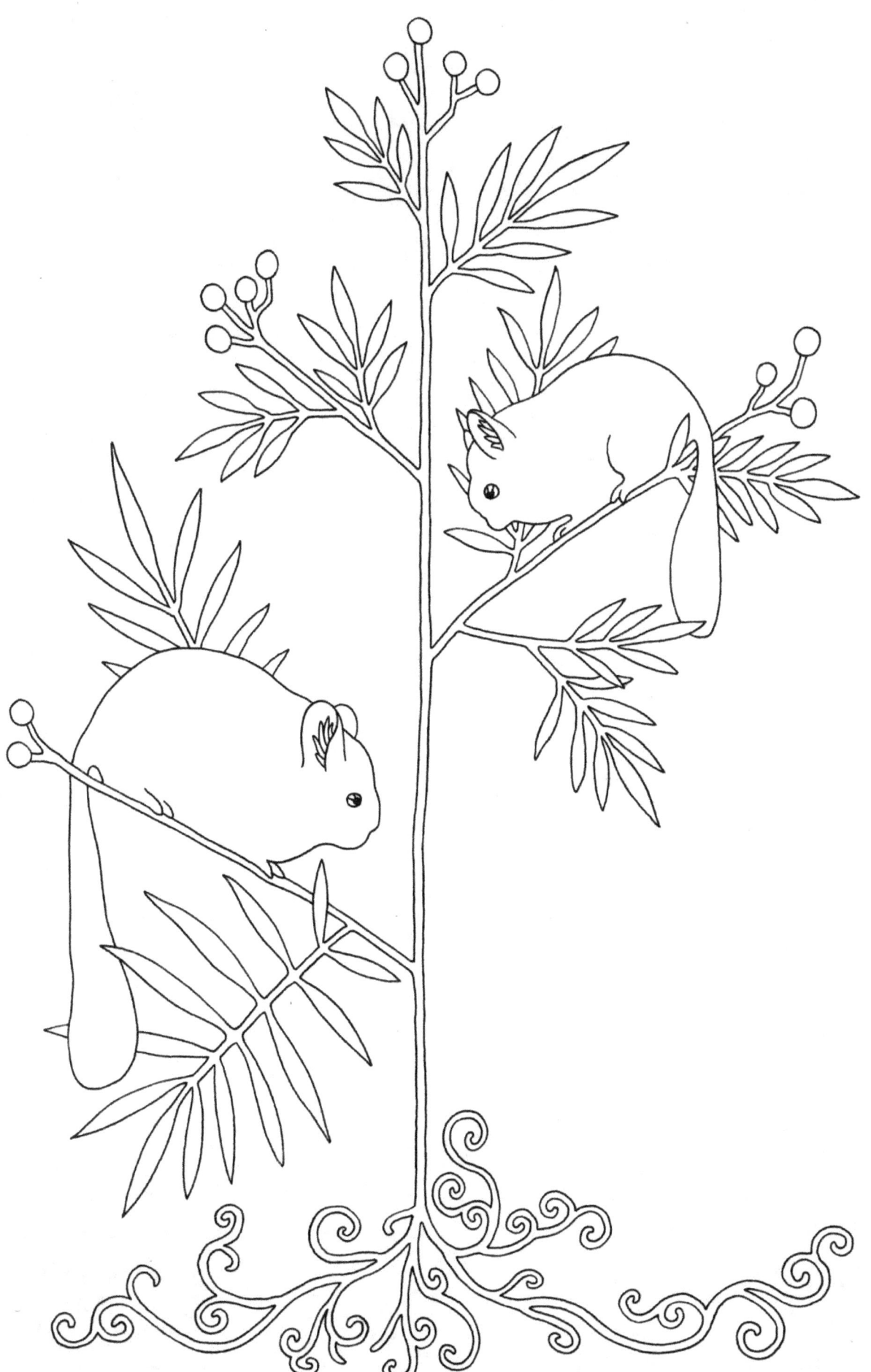

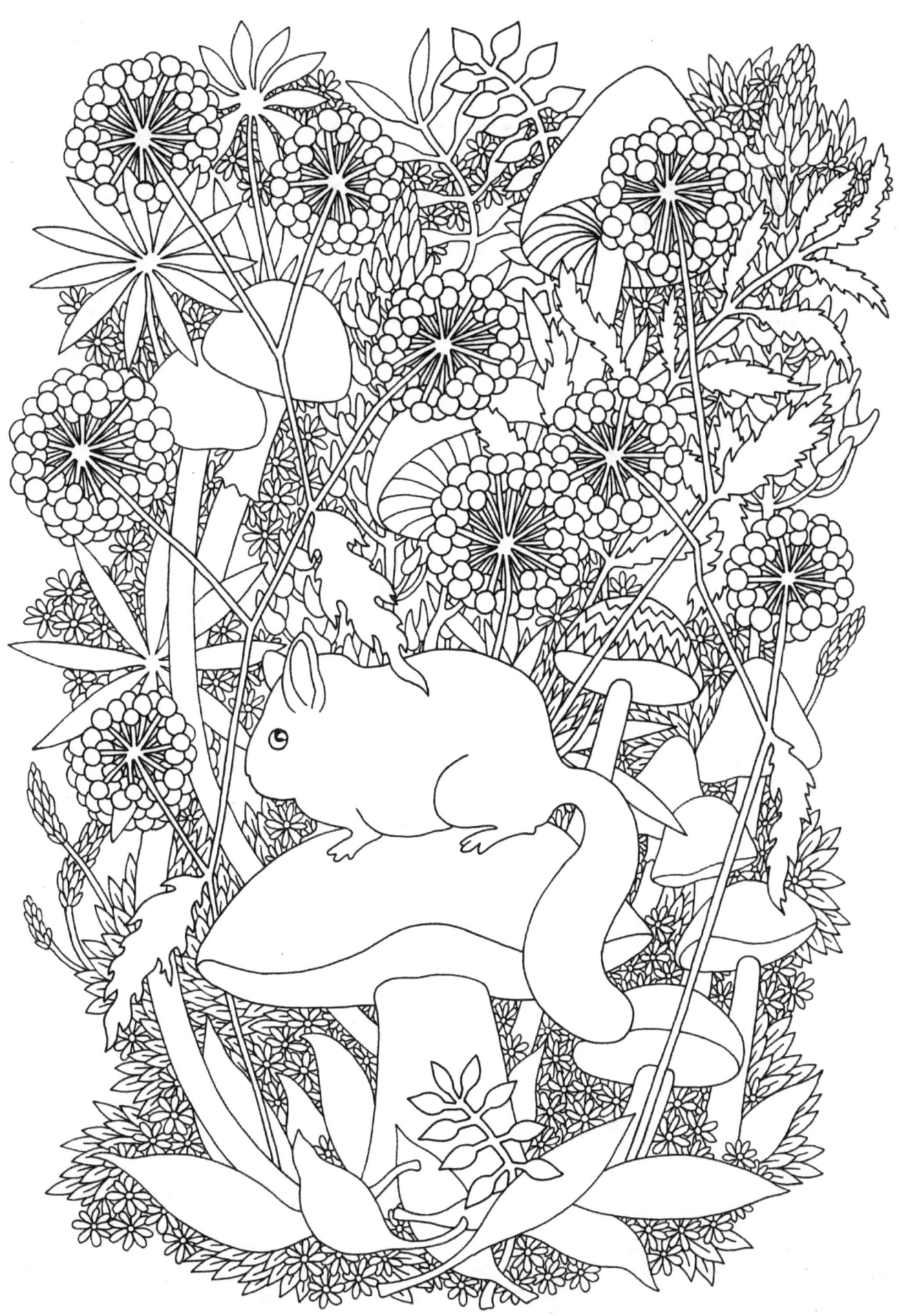

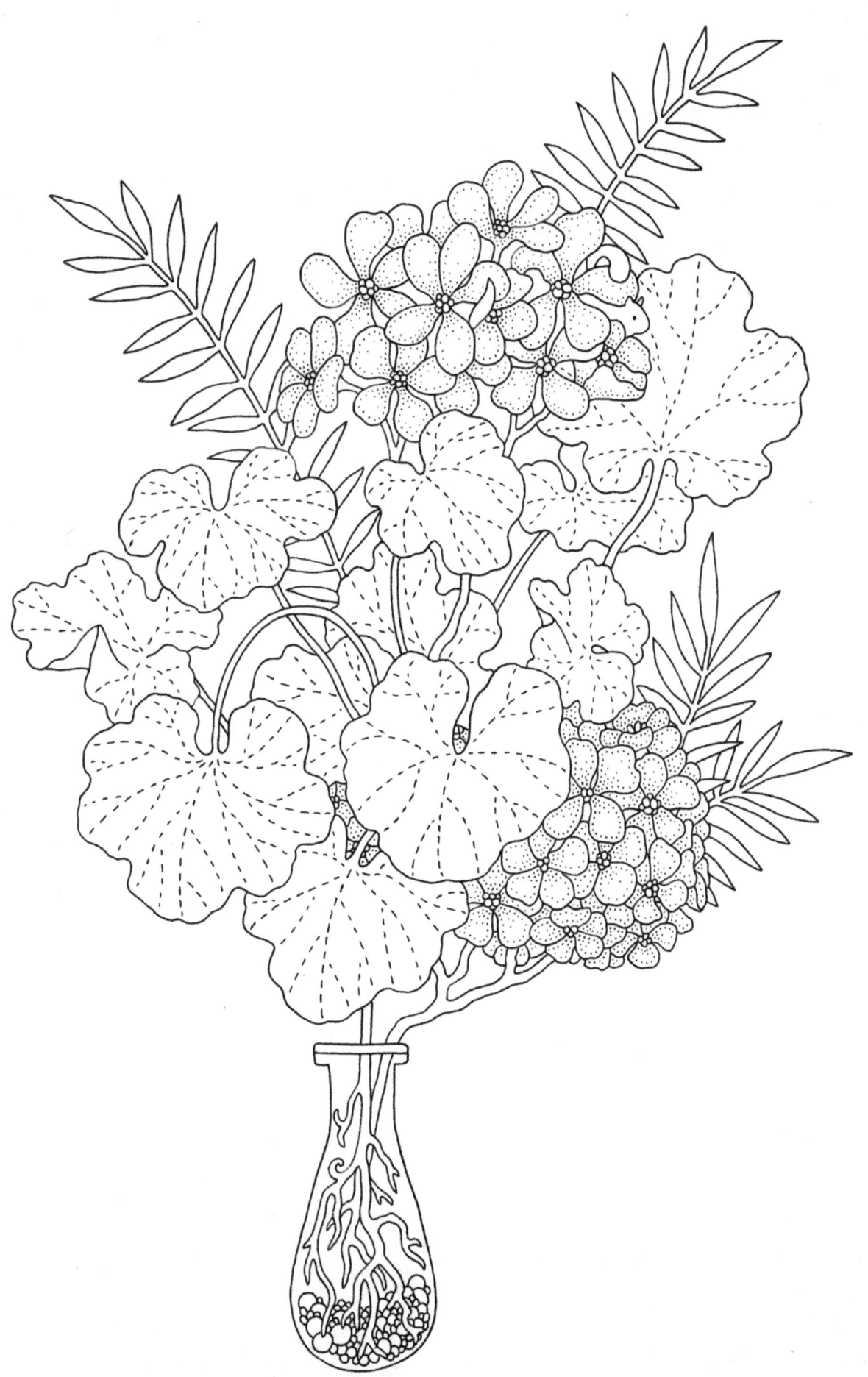

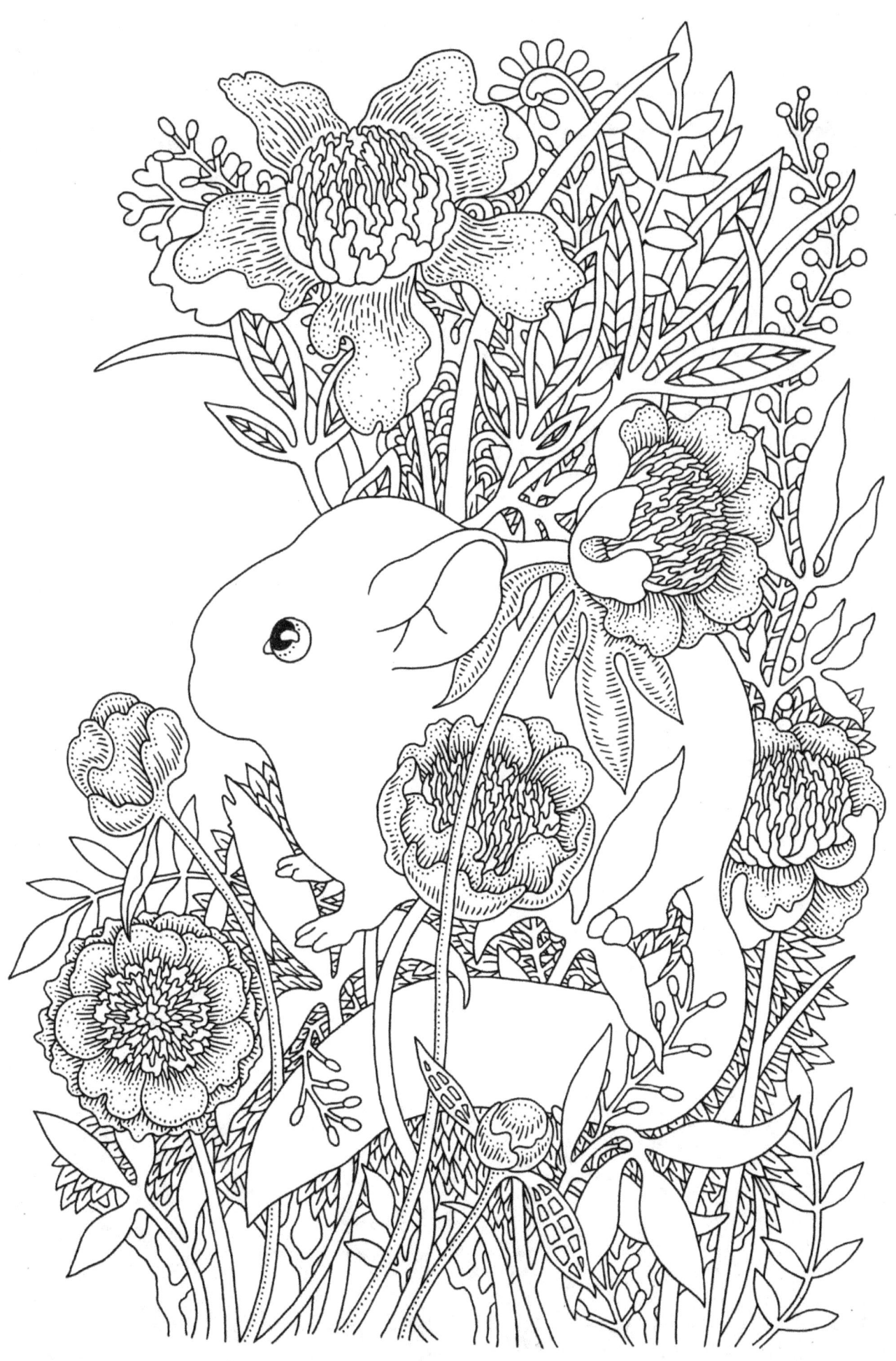

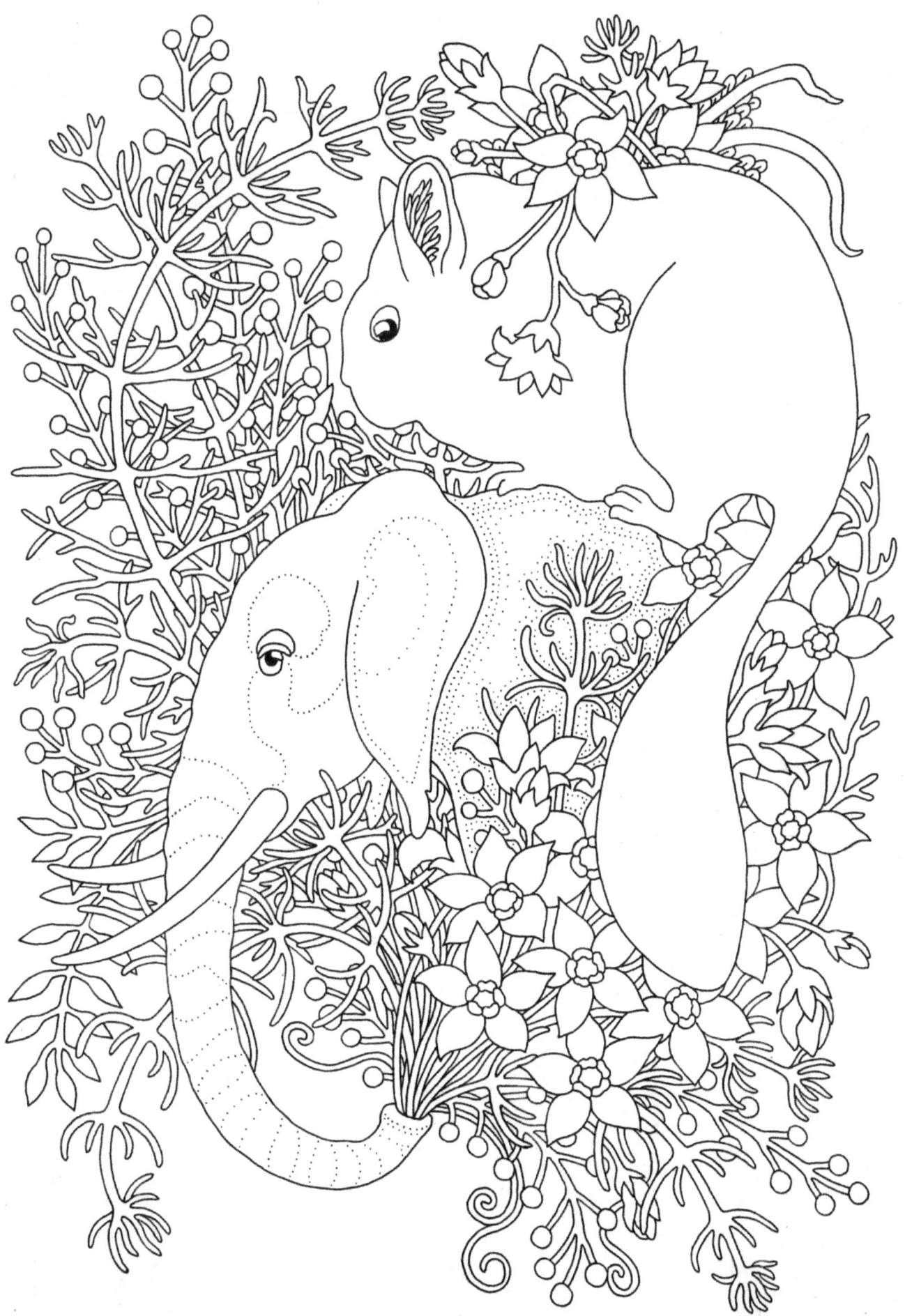

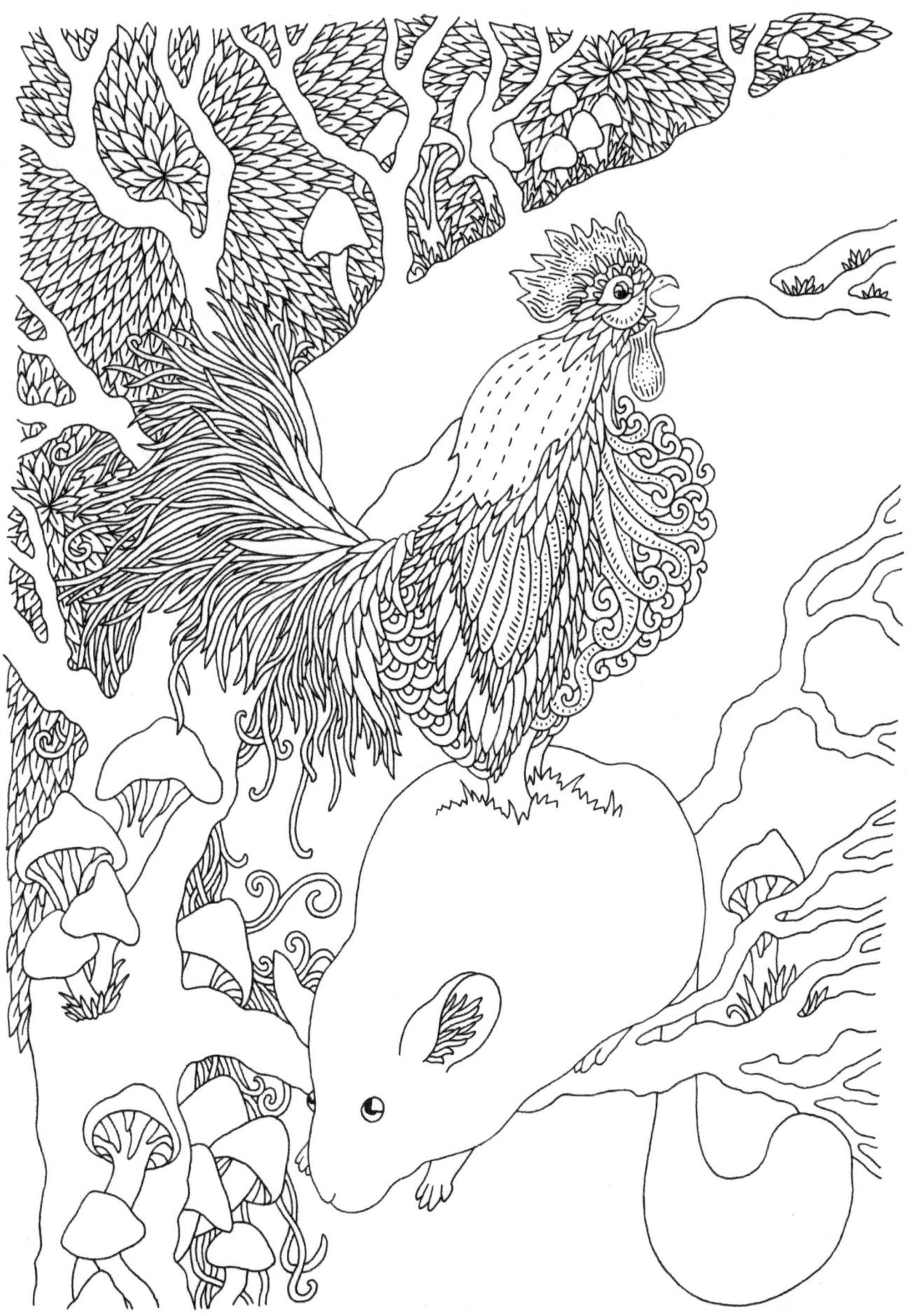

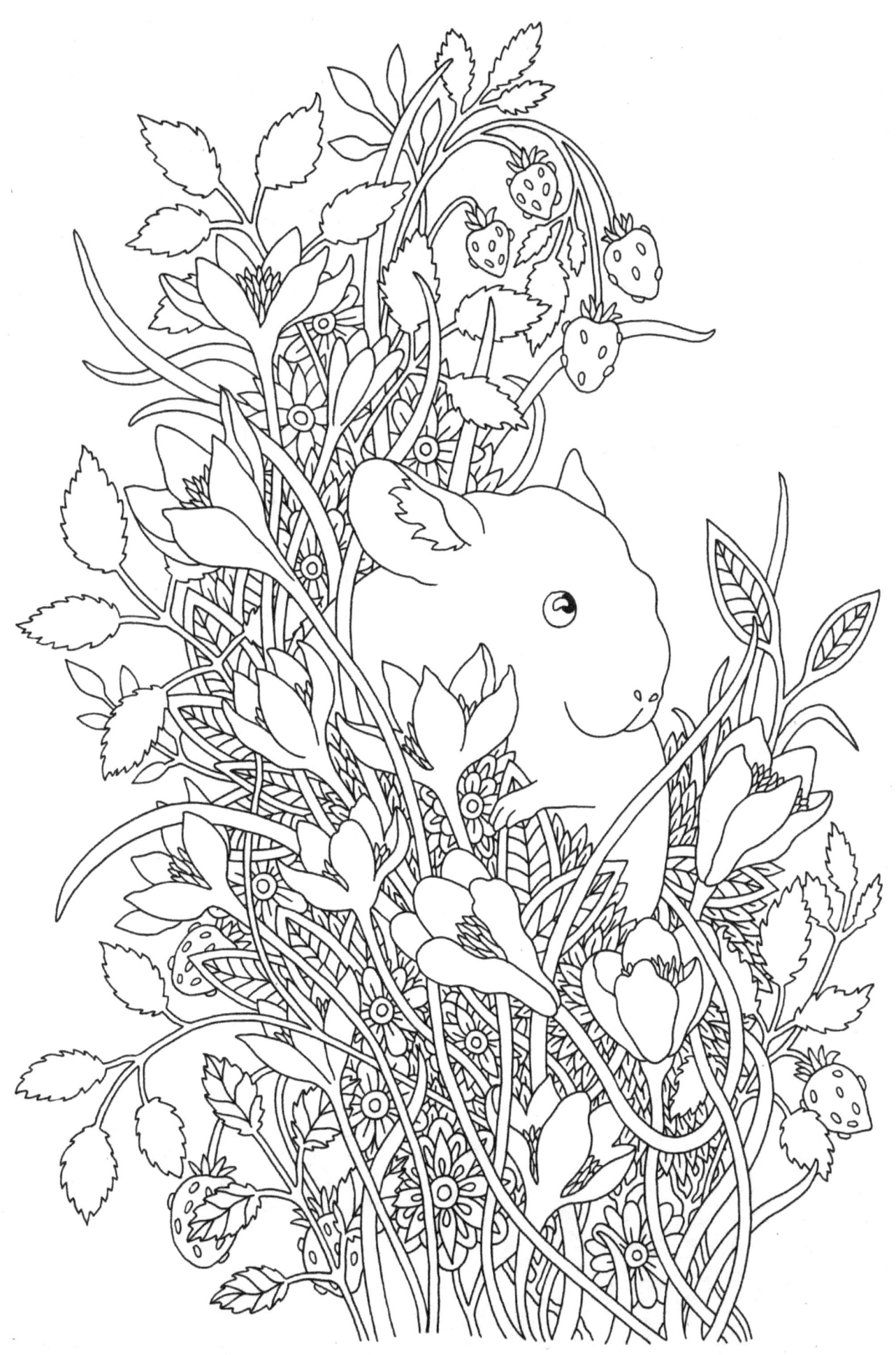

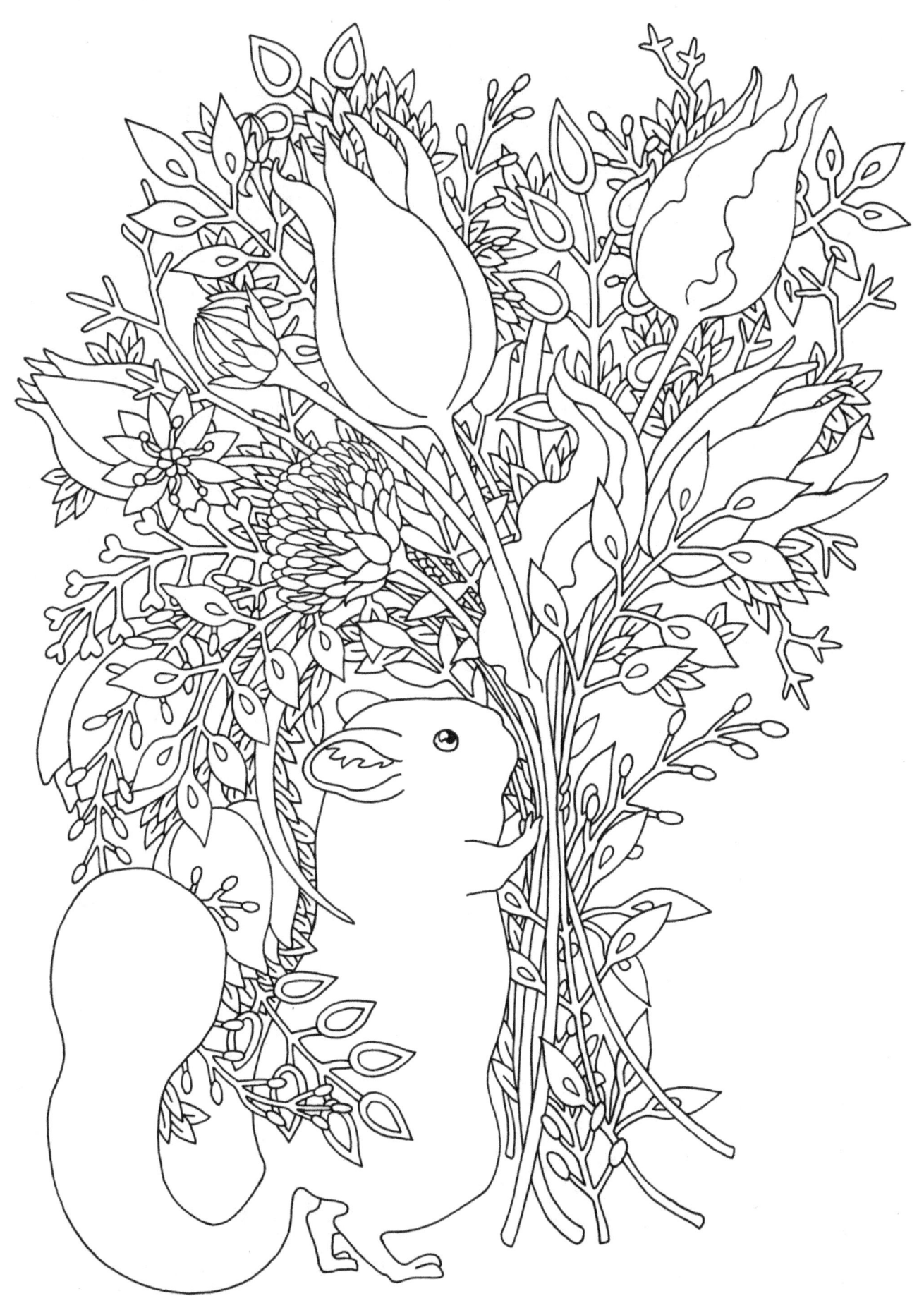

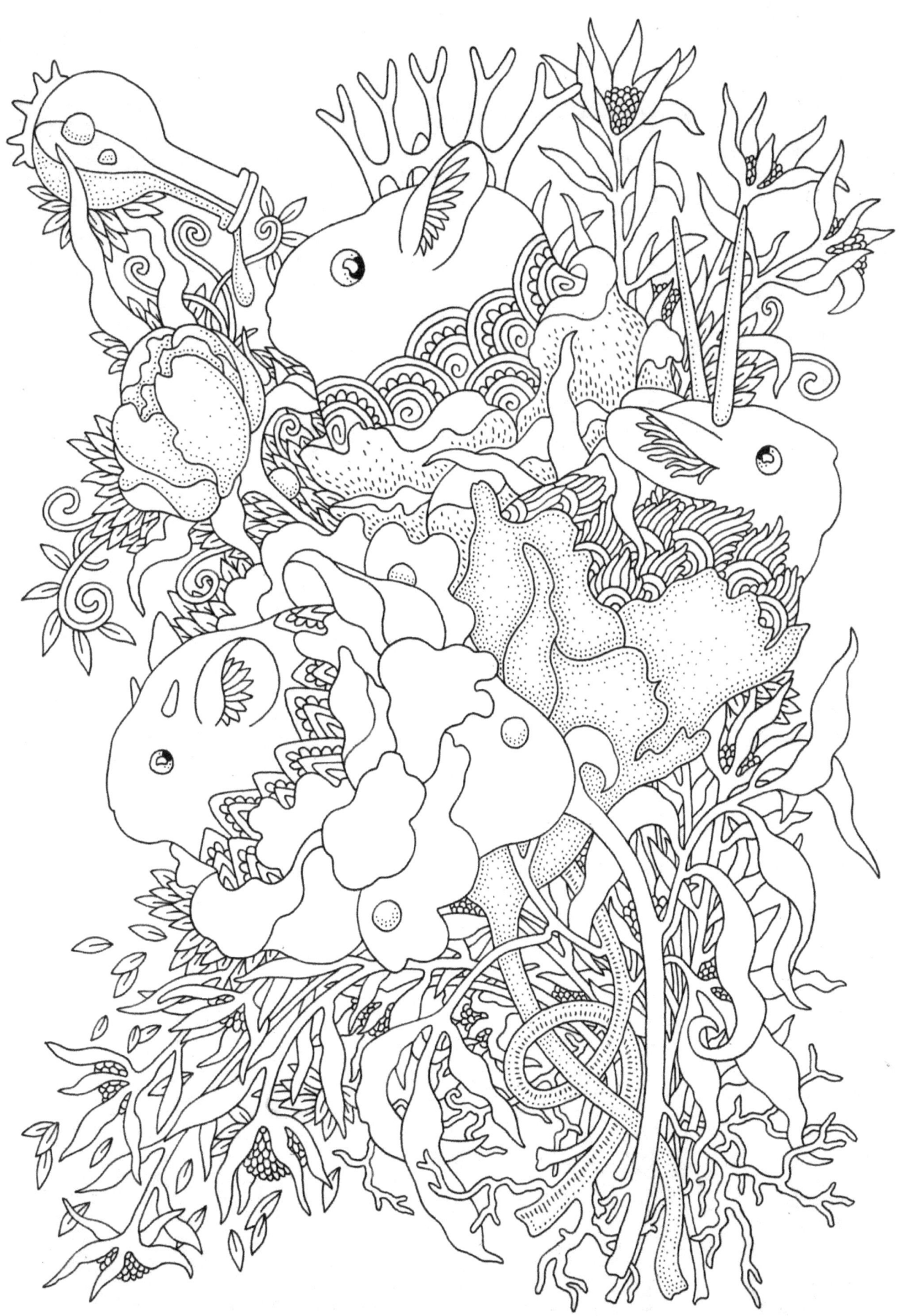

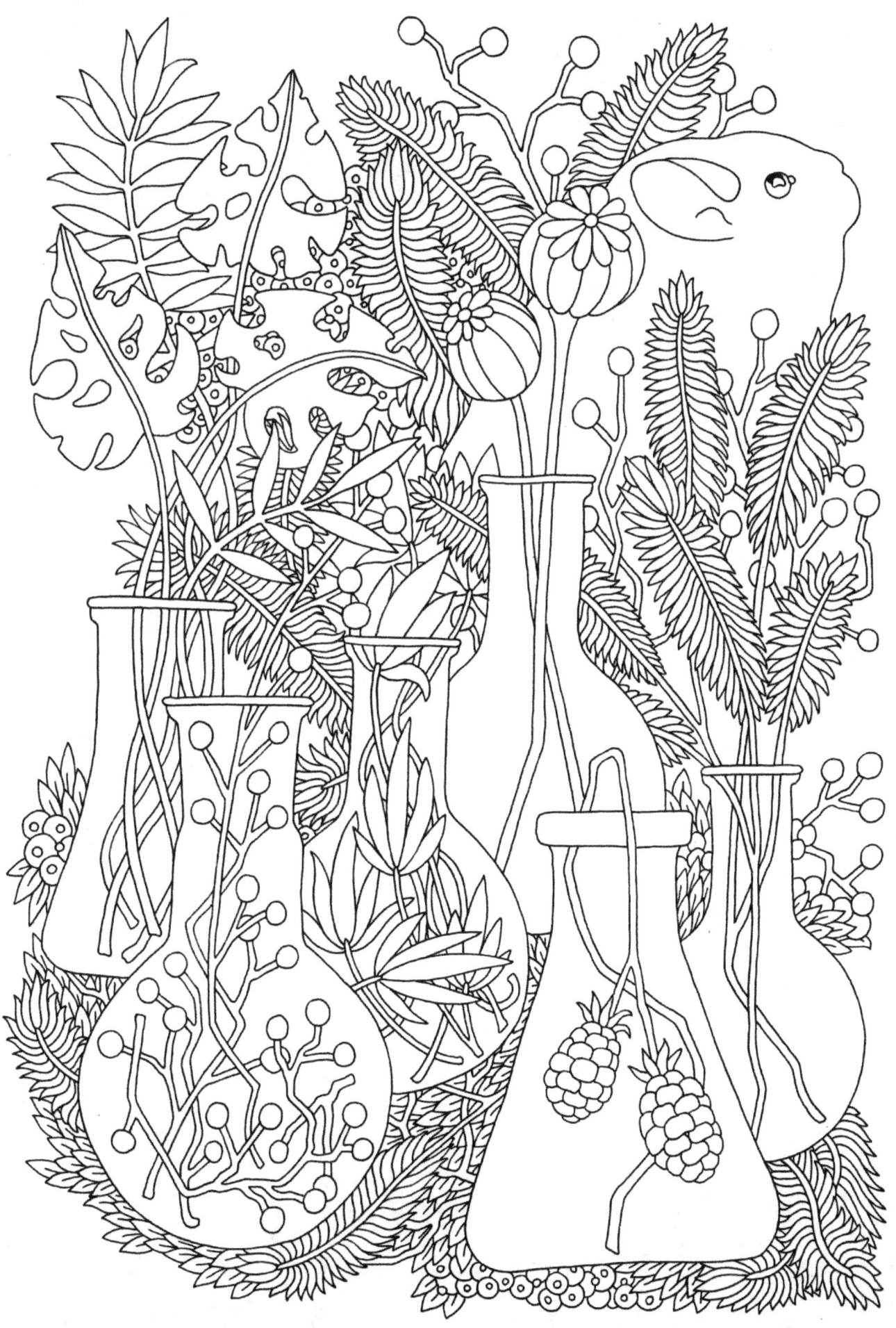

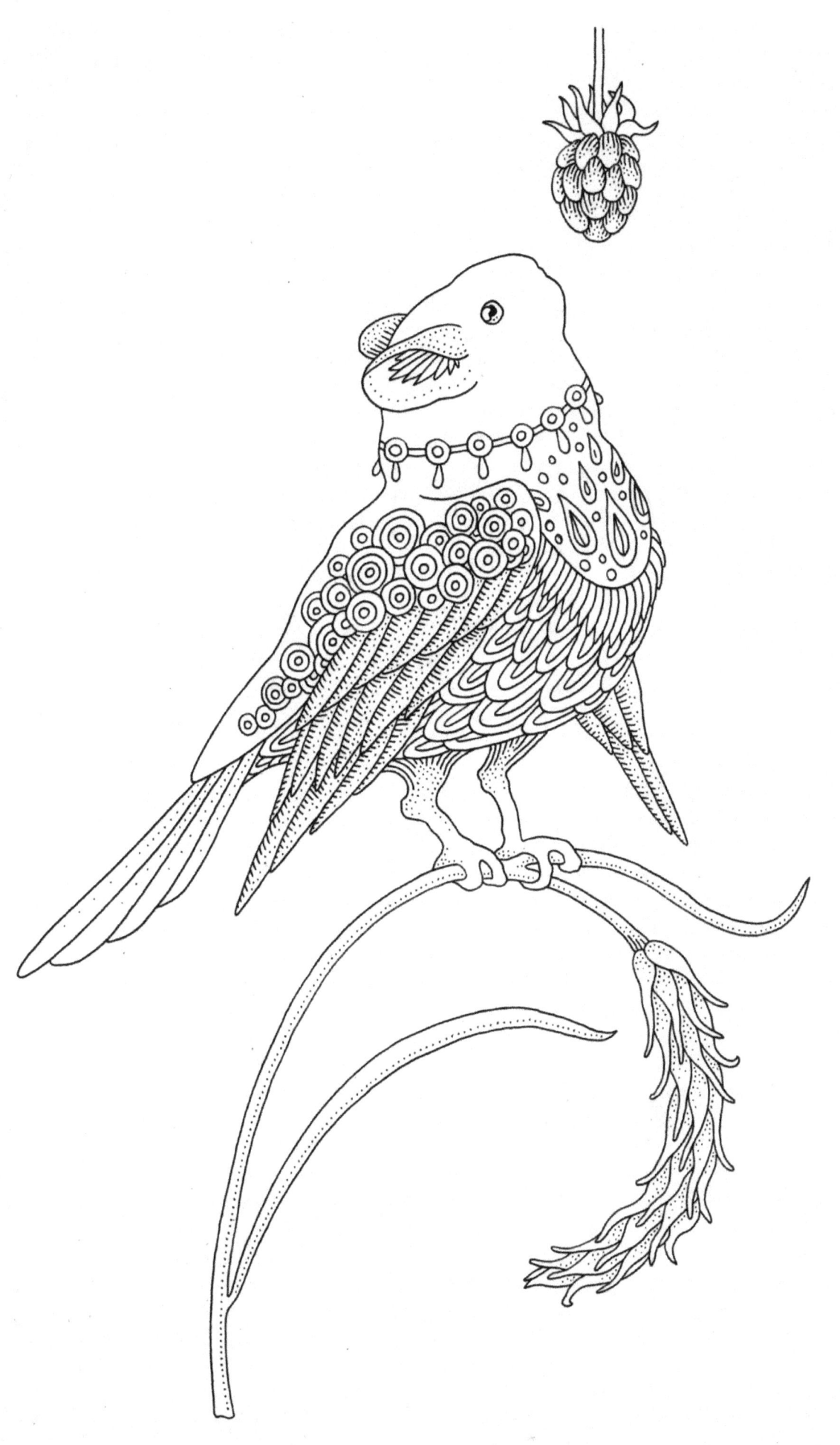

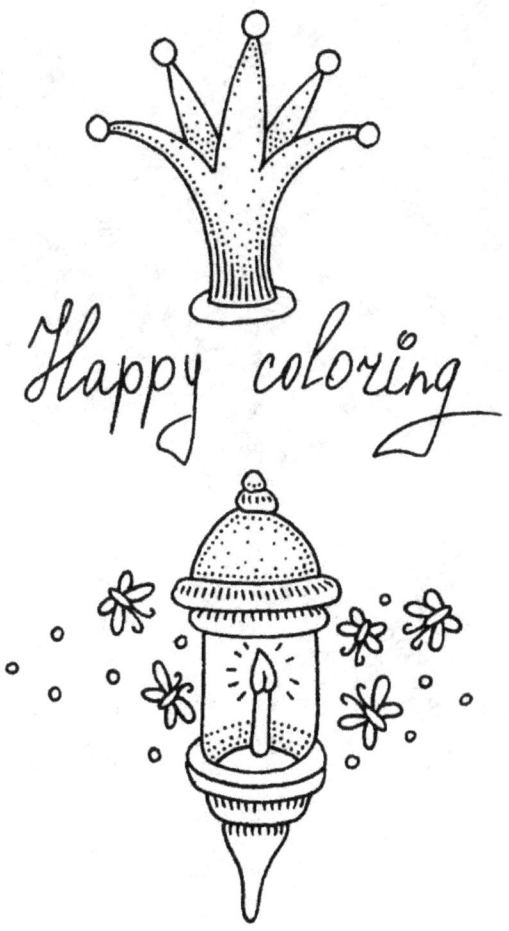

Happy coloring

Thank you for choosing
my coloring book!

Olya :)

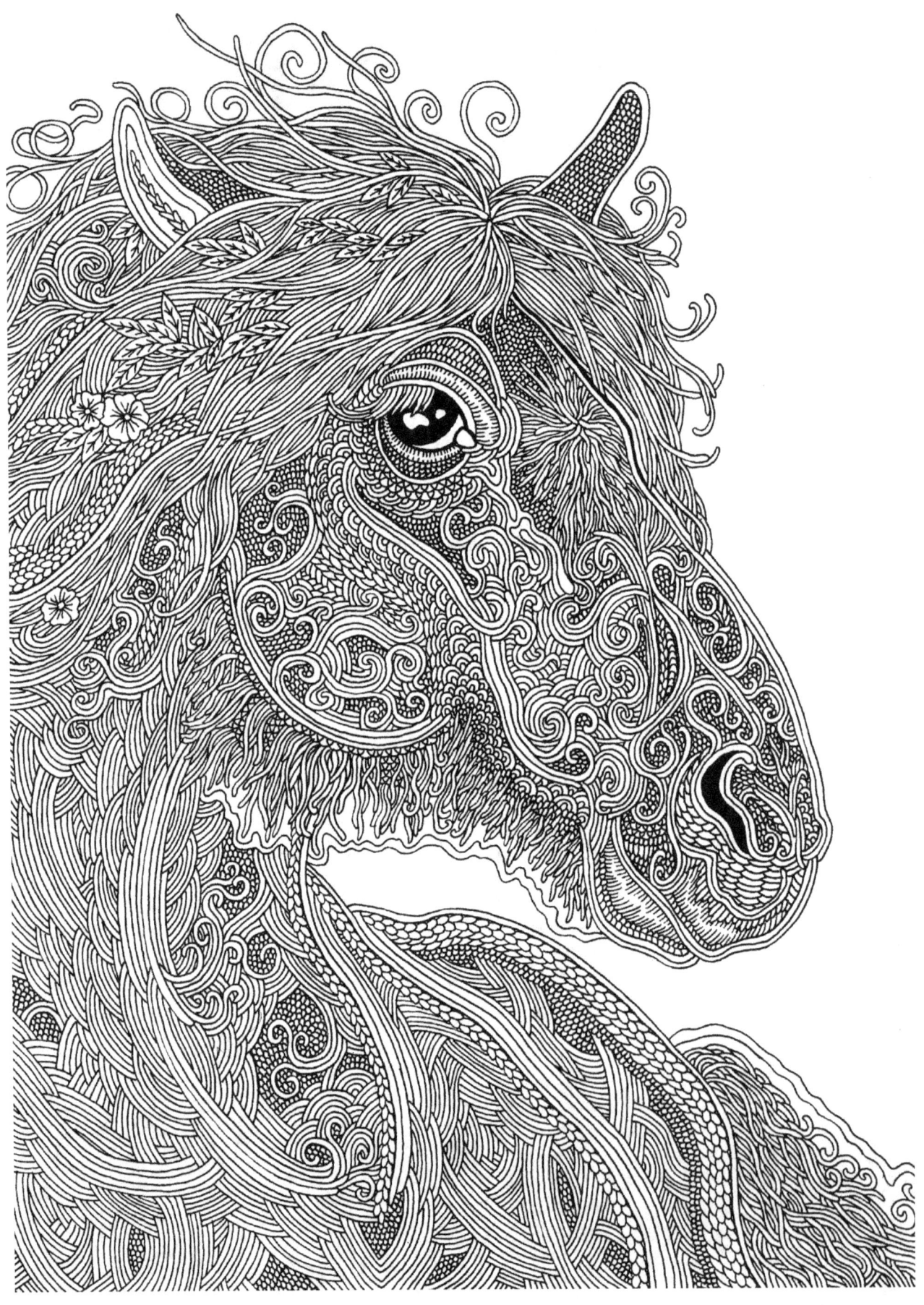

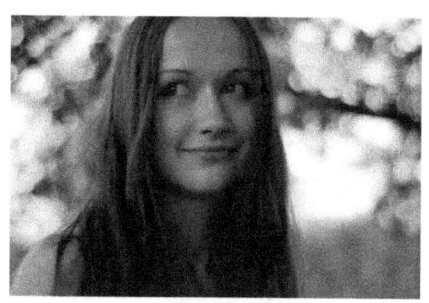

ABOUT THE AUTHOR

Olga Goloveshkina is a freelance artist and illustrator based in Moscow, Russia.
She graduated from the Institute of Business and Design.
Olga specializes in black ink doodles.
She is an author and illustrator coloring books for adults:
1. "The wind carries flowers"/"Veter unosit tsvety" (in Russian, 2015),
2. "Fox travel: Coloring book" (in English, 2016),
3. "Mounts" (in English, 2016),
4. "Mounts 2" (in English, 2016),
5. "Enchanted horses" (in English, 2016),
6. "Horse and Architecture" (in English, 2016),
7. "Alice in Wonderland Coloring Book" (in English, 2017),
8. "Mounts 3" zodiac coloring book (in English, 2017),
9. "Mounts 4" Halloween coloring book (in English, 2017),
10. "Mounts 5" Christmas coloring book (in English, 2017),
11. "The queens. Monsters. Werewolves. Goddesses." (in English, 2018),
12. "Chinchilla Art Journal Coloring Book" (in English, 2018).

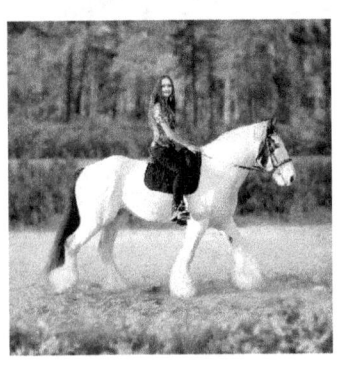

AUTHOR PAGE ON AMAZON:
AMAZON.COM/AUTHOR/OLGAGOLOVESHKINA

SITE: HTTP://OLYAGOLOVESHKINA.JIMDO.COM

ETSY.COM/SHOP/OLYACOLORINGBOOK

INSTAGRAM:
@OLYAHITRAYAPANDA

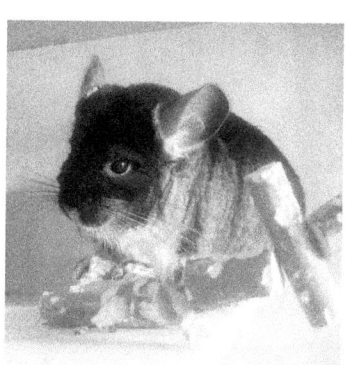

INSTAGRAM:
@PERCHIK_THE_CHINCHILLA
#CHINCHILLAARTJOURNAL

www.ingramcontent.com/pod-product-compliance
Lightning Source LLC
Chambersburg PA
CBHW081747220526
45468CB00008B/2281